Praise for *The Se*

D1124841

"*The Secret Lives of Teen Girls* is a bold and much needed
perspective on teen sexuality and should be a must read for all parents
of teens. Evelyn's patient stories and personal experiences provide
real-world examples that help readers relate to the challenges mothers
and daughters face during adolescence. I have been a women's
health care provider for over 25 years and plan to
recommend this book to parents seeking guidance."

— **Carrie Klima, Ph.D.**, **CNM**, University of Illinois
at Chicago, College of Nursing

"*I laughed aloud and bemoaned that I hadn't read
The Secret Lives of Teen Girls before my daughter's
adolescence arrived. With wisdom, grace, and an endearing sense
of humor, Evelyn Resh encourages a mother to just say yes to her
daughter's emerging sexual, relational, and uniquely independent
self. Both informative and entertaining, it's sure to resonate with
mothers, who dance on the head of a pin as they try to help their
daughters negotiate the joys of becoming women.*"

— **Renée Schultz**, co-author,
The Mother-Daughter Project

"*An honest, cogent, indispensible guide that sparkles with insights
for parents, grandparents, teachers, counselors, and everyone who cares
about teenage girls. Evelyn Resh tackles the sexual dramas and paradoxes
of growing up with sound medical advice and teachable 'Aha!'
moments that offer galaxies more than 'just say no.'*"

— **Gina Ogden, Ph.D.**, author of *Women Who Love Sex, The Heart
and Soul of Sex*, and *The Return of Desire*

"*Whether or not we know it, Evelyn Resh's **The Secret Lives of
Teen Girls** is a resource we all have been waiting for. Her insights
about adolescent girls' sexuality, maternal fears and anxiety, and the
intricate relationship between the two are clearly and honestly discussed
in this brave new book. Sharing examples that demonstrate the sometimes
frightening aspects of adolescent rebellion, Ms. Resh offers timely advice
that can help mothers take the bold steps to honor their daughters' choices
and accept their mistakes. The author's wisdom about adolescent girls'
sexuality, tempered with humor and sensitivity, makes this book
essential reading for every mother of a teenage girl.*"

— **Catriona McHardy**, Vice President of Education & Training,
Planned Parenthood of Northern New England

the secret lives of TEEN GIRLS

the
secret lives of
TEEN GIRLS

What Your Mother Wouldn't Talk about but Your Daughter Needs to Know

Evelyn K. Resh, CNM, MPH

with Beverly West

HAY HOUSE, INC.
Carlsbad, California • New York City
London • Sydney • Johannesburg
Vancouver • Hong Kong • New Delhi

Published and distributed in the United States by: Hay House, Inc.: www.hayhouse.com • *Published and distributed in Australia by:* Hay House Australia Pty. Ltd.: www.hayhouse.com.au • *Published and distributed in the United Kingdom by:* Hay House UK, Ltd.: www .hayhouse.co.uk • *Published and distributed in the Republic of South Africa by:* Hay House SA (Pty), Ltd.: www.hayhouse.co.za • *Distributed in Canada by:* Raincoast: www.raincoast.com • *Published in India by:* Hay House Publishers India: www.hayhouse.co.in

Design: Jen Kennedy

Library of Congress Cataloging-in-Publication Data

Resh, Evelyn K.
  The secret lives of teen girls : what your mother wouldn't talk about, but your daughter needs to know / Evelyn K. Resh, with Beverly West. -- 1st ed.
      p. cm.
  Includes bibliographical references.
  ISBN 978-1-4019-2278-8 (pbk. : alk. paper) 1. Teenage girls--Sexual behavior. I. West, Beverly, 1961- II. Title.
  HQ27.5.R47 2009
  613.9'55--dc22
                                    2009018933

ISBN: 978-1-4019-2278-8

12 11 10 09   4 3 2 1
1st edition, September 2009

Printed in the United States of America

For my daughter, Thalia,

My best teacher, granter of insights, mender of wounds
With so much love

*"Girls live and grow up in bodies that
are capable of strong sexual feelings, bodies that are
connected to minds and hearts that hold meanings
through which they make sense of and perceive their bodies.
I consider the possibility that teenage girls' sexual desire
is important and life sustaining; that girls' desire provides
crucial information about the relational world in which they
live; that societal obstacles to girls' and women's ability to
feel and act on their own desire should come under
scrutiny rather than simply be feared; that girls and
women are entitled to have sexual subjectivity,
rather than simply to be sexual objects."*

— Deborah L. Tolman, *Dilemmas of Desire:
Teenage Girls Talk about Sexuality*

*"It didn't seem fair to her that a girl's virginity
was so prized when a boy's was merely a burden
to unload at the first opportunity."*

— Cristina Garcia, *A Handbook to Luck*

CONTENTS

INTRODUCTION

RAISING APHRODITE

"Some say a squadron of horse, some, infantry,
Some, ships, are the loveliest thing
On the black earth. But I say
It's what you desire."

— Sappho

The Secret Lives of Teen Girls is my attempt to better understand how the sexual feelings, experiences, and education of adolescent girls I treat as a midwife relate to the sexual, emotional, and physical problems of the adult women I advise in my sexuality counseling practice. I hope to use this understanding to help my own teenage daughter (who happens to be pictured on the front of this book) and teenage girls everywhere to grow into sexually healthy adult women, capable of enjoying a fulfilling and satisfying sexual life with the loving partner of their choice.

Writing a book about the importance of sex in the lives of teen girls and the problems with sex that many women report seems to be the best way to convey to others what I have found to be true in my practice; sex is more important to teen girls than we think or say it is, and their experiences in adolescence correlate with and influence their feelings and decisions about sex through-out adulthood. This book will bring you into my world, which has afforded me the enormous opportunity to hear how girls and women feel and experience their sexuality—beginning in adolescence, and how those experiences translate into their adult lives.

I became a certified nurse-midwife after practicing as a registered nurse on a busy maternity unit of a community hospital in western Massachusetts, where my practice included a diverse population and many teenage girls. I had always assumed that being a midwife would be primarily about delivering babies. I never imagined that a large part of my practice would include becoming counselor, confidante, and advocate for teenage girls who were coping with critical problems like unplanned pregnancies, domestic violence, rape, substance abuse, sexually transmitted infections, AIDS, depression, self-mutilation, eating disorders, and homelessness—to name just a few. Others were dealing with less serious but still troubling issues like underachievement, poor school performance, low self-esteem, combative relationships with their parents, and chronic moodiness.

As a health professional, I became frustrated and a little bewildered about the often needless dramas that I saw unfolding every day in my examining room. This frustration led me to ask some tough questions. Why was I diagnosing so many 14-year-olds with STIs? Why were girls cutting themselves, starving themselves, and courting disaster by having unsafe sex? When did the fashion sense of 13-year-olds become so sexually explicit? Why were most teenage girls so bent on keeping secrets from their parents? And why weren't moms reaching out to their daughters and talking to them about what was really going on?

I did talk to my young patients about what was really going on, and I listened to their stories, and I began to realize that these girls, regardless of their circumstances or health status, had two important things in common. They were all struggling with problems that arose primarily from the fact that they were coping with the new and sudden emergence of their sexuality, and almost without exception, these girls were being left to develop a sexual identity alone, without any help or guidance from their parents or teachers, and often without even the most basic knowledge about what was happening to them physically or emotionally.

My patients' emerging sexuality and sexual activity were a lightning rod for their parents' distress. In other words, when confronted with the reality of their daughters' sexual feelings, most parents either became enraged, started yelling, or shut down—ignoring the subject of sex completely. Day in and day out, I witnessed firsthand what was happening to my young patients whose feelings, life experiences, mistakes, or even plain old normal adolescent behavior went unguided, untended to, denied, or simply misunderstood by well-intentioned parents who were uncomfortable with their daughters' sexuality. As a result, they were ultimately unable to parent their daughters at all through this crucial phase of their development.

Make no mistake about it. Leaving teenage girls alone to cope with the many serious and sometimes life-threatening issues related to sex and the development of their sexual identity is a foolproof recipe for disaster. At the very least, it makes difficult situations much more complicated and, perhaps, life changing.

At this point, I began to ask some tougher questions, and not of my patients, but of myself. Why do we moms, and society as a whole, have such a huge problem with teenage girls becoming sexual? After all, it happened to many of us as teenagers, too. Why don't we ever focus on the good things about our daughters' sexual development? Why do we clam up, turn away, hit the panic button, or start shouting, instead of offering our teenage daughters the benefit of our own sexual history and knowledge, in the hopes that we can make their first sexual experiences as positive, healthful, and enjoyable as possible? And why, when we, as a culture, put so much focus on our children's professional, spiritual, and intellectual development, do we leave our kids completely on their own to bushwhack their way through the wilderness of their sexual development without the benefit of a parental compass?

Understandably, when we parents think of our teen girls becoming desirable, sexually active creatures, our minds immediately turn to the risks of STIs, unplanned pregnancies, broken hearts, and tainted reputations. Confronted with these very real risks, many of us immediately start preaching abstinence with a fury, hoping to stave off disaster, or cover our eyes and hope that our daughters' sexual energy and interests will just go away. These were the very same strategies that most of us experienced with our own parents when we were teenagers. Although our research data on teens and their sexual activity is limited, according to current statistics, 47.8 percent of high school students reported having had intercourse.[1] And a report published by the Guttmacher Institute shows that more than 750,000 girls between the ages of 15–19 become pregnant annually.[2] Although this rate of teen pregnancies is the lowest it's been in 30 years, it remains one of the highest in the developing world.

It's understandable, in light of these statistics, that we warn our daughters about the risks and dangers of partnered sex, hoping that our "just say no" message will stick. The facts about teenage sex, however, clearly demonstrate that oftentimes our daughters don't or can't say no to Mother Nature and that anger, denial, threats, and morality are poor defenses against the forces of biology.

This is not to say that girls should be encouraged to say yes to partnered sex as the spirit moves them. But the fact is that they often do and they have legitimate reasons for doing so, reasons that we as parents often invalidate and disallow. Out of fear, we lose sight of the bigger picture of what sex really represents for teenage girls: individuation and growth into fully developed adult women capable of seeking and finding pleasure with a loving and supportive partner.

Teens need to be allowed to be exactly who they are: young people, driven by an abundance of physical and emotional energy that directs them toward intimacy and sex as a means to become independent young adults who have successfully separated from their parents. When we interrupt this natural process by denying it, or attempting to suppress it, we risk doing damage to our daughters' development—damage that could potentially affect their emotional and physical health for a lifetime.

While there are unquestionably dangers associated with teenagers having sex, there are also dangers to be considered when teenagers deny their sexual feelings and fail to act or at least consider their growing urges.

While we may feel that we are protecting our children by teaching them to postpone acting on their sexual feelings until they are adults, we are in fact retarding their development, which opens them up to a whole new host of difficulties.

Refusing to acknowledge, support, and encourage our daughters' developing sexual identity and the feelings of desire and longing associated with this gives our daughters the message that their feelings, and the feeling state in general, are irrelevant. Further, refusing to discuss sex with our daughters becomes a major roadblock to open communication between girls and their mothers, which can greatly increase the hazards for girls in adolescence. And not allowing our daughters to begin making their own emotional and sexual decisions in adolescence can interfere with their ability to make sound, safe, and independent decisions throughout their lives.

Finally, and perhaps most important, consistently giving our daughters the message that sex is only about reproductive hazards and the dangers of STIs and pregnancy sets them up for a life in which they don't think about sexuality from a pleasure perspective at all. This lack of guidance during such a critical part of our daughters' development does not instill or encourage the formation of a pleasure paradigm in their lives. For some girls, this can result in a lifelong inability to seek out sexual satisfaction and pleasure within intimate relationships. For others, it encourages lifelong promiscuity with random partners. Either way, avoiding the subject of sex and expecting our daughters to do the same thing is the best way to ensure that we will raise sexually unhealthy and relationally unfulfilled adult women.

Currently, as Director of Sexual Health Services and Programming at Canyon Ranch Health Resort in Lenox, Massachusetts, I care for adult women who come to see me about their sexual struggles and difficulties achieving fulfilling relationships with their partners. My patients tell me repeatedly that they believe that their problems were in large part the result of the ways in which their emerging sexuality was treated in adolescence. They tell me about the sexual terrorism imposed on them by parents in misguided efforts to keep them safe, including the shame they were made to feel by parents who simply didn't know any better.

Adolescence is the time when romantic love often blooms and girls are immersed in the discovery of their own beauty, sexual appeal, and bravado. Unfortunately, they are also frequently humiliated, punished, and restrained by their parents for something that occurs naturally and is often beyond their control. Instead of emerging from adolescence with a vibrancy of spirit that can energize and inform their adult lives, they learn to drive their sensual pleasures, longings, and appetites underground and keep them secret from everyone, including themselves. By the time they reach adulthood, they have no real internal compass that can point them in the direction of pleasure and relational fulfillment.

The sad truth is that most of us paid a dear price for behaving in ways as teens that were part of our normal development. The sadder truth is that things haven't changed much over the years. We continue to make the same mistakes with our own daughters that our parents made with us—mistakes rooted in the denial of the role that sexuality plays in our individuation and maturation from teens into adults.

The Secret Lives of Teen Girls is my attempt to illustrate and define the true significance and value of the sexual feelings and experiences of teenage girls and the potentially lifelong hazards our daughters face when parents deny or simply fail to acknowledge these feelings. To help readers better understand these issues, in addition to sharing my insights about the links between adolescent sexuality and lifelong sexual health, I have included a list of questions at the end of each chapter. Use them to gain deeper insight into your own feelings about sex (in adolescence and as an adult) and how these feelings may be affecting the way you parent your daughter. There is also a Resources section at the end of the book that may be helpful to you. It is my intention that the information you glean from your answers and the resources will help dispel the pervasive myth that sexual activity in teen girls is inherently bad, risky, and always misguided. I also hope your answers will help you parent in more loving and effective ways and with an eye toward your daughter's sexual health and satisfaction throughout life. Teen sex is not the most serious problem we face as parents, nor is it the riskiest thing girls face as teens. It's the secrets we keep from our teenagers about sex, and the secrets we force them to keep from us, that do our daughters the greatest harm.

CHAPTER 1

THE SECRET CHEMISTRY OF DESIRE

"When I searched the literature to find out what psychologists knew about girls' sexual desire, I found that no one had asked about it. In the many hundreds of studies that have been done to determine what predicts adolescent girl's sexual behavior, only a handful had identified girls' sexual desire as a potential factor."

— Deborah L. Tolman, *Dilemmas of Desire*

How does it happen? One day, seemingly out of the clear blue sky, your darling daughter miraculously transforms into a full-fledged vixen. She no longer walks, she prowls, and she's got a look in her eyes that you think you recognize but hoped you'd never see. The look is flat out sexy—or at least trying to be—and to go along with it is a demanding, sullen, and unpredictable disposition. And she's wearing outfits so tiny you need your reading glasses to see them. This is panic material for parents, especially mothers. And, as moms will do, our first instinct is to give our daughters the benefit of the doubt, reassuring ourselves with thoughts like *Surely, my daughter isn't acting as sexy as she looks,* or *Surely she has no clue about what she is really doing.*

If you are one of the many mothers who think and feel this way, your interpretations are only partially accurate. While your daughter herself may be completely innocent about what is happening, your daughter's body knows exactly what she's doing. Your daughter is becoming a woman, which entails a tidal wave of change that will involve her physical, psychological, emotional, and spiritual being. All these changes are necessary for her to eventually become a fully engaged, actualized, and sexually active and mature adult woman. And all of these changes begin to take hold when she first experiences the transformational chemistry of desire.

Sexual energy and desire are extraordinarily powerful physical and emotional sensations which lead people of all ages into having partnered sex. Some of the choices and decisions we make about whom to have sex with are wiser and safer than others. For those of us parenting teen girls, the thought of our immature and impulsive daughters wrangling with such intense physical and emotional longings is frightening! The terror we experience can render us immobile, unhelpful, critical, and sometimes even hurtful as mothers, much as many of our own mothers were toward us. But it doesn't have to be this way. Making an effort to understand more about the forces at work in the body and brain of teenage girls will make it easier for mothers to participate more actively and comfortably in their daughters' lives as they develop their sexual identities and at the same time permit their daughters to grow and develop into safe and satisfied sexual adults.

Teenage girls are strongly influenced by their biology and their hormones. As much as we might like them to, teens really can't just say no to Mother Nature when it comes to sex, because this is part of their natural development. In order to have a better understanding of what's actually happening physically in the alchemy of desire, let's take a closer look at the biological changes that occur in girls during their teens.

Puberty is defined in medicine and human development as the phase during which human beings develop secondary sex characteristics and subsequently acquire the physical maturation and ability to conceive and reproduce. For teen girls, this means their breasts develop; body fat increases around the abdomen, buttocks, and hips; pubic hair grows; their ovaries begin releasing eggs to be fertilized, thereby allowing them to conceive and deliver a baby. On first pass this sounds like a straightforward and simple shift along the course of human development. However, the translation in the real life of humans is more like the all-hell-breaking-loose phase. I think of it as the time in our daughters' lives when being a parent is filled with terror and when our sanity and ability to cope with life stressors are maximally challenged.

When we consider the social context in which puberty occurs, the responsibilities and hazards associated with it, and the emotions that are generated by the increase in hormones that causes this avalanche, there's really nothing simple or subtle about it. The changes that occur in the body and the brain at this time are vast, dramatic, influential, and undeniable. This is a time in our lives as parents when we are at the complete mercy of nature. Most of us both dread and fear the foreseeable future and would rather send our girls to another planet for a few years than live with them.

THE MAGIC THREE

The steady and low levels of the hormones estrogen, progesterone, and testosterone—what I call the Magic Three—prior to puberty make for gradual changes in our daughters as they grow up. In a normal course of childhood, most parents can sit back and enjoy the transformation of a first grader to a second grader (and so on) with relatively few freak-outs. Sometimes tantrums and unpleasant phases occur and might last longer than we feel is reasonable. But in general, these unpleasant episodes are short lived and the radius of potential negative impact on self and others is limited. Being a parent during this time is pretty much smooth sailing.

Once puberty occurs around age 12, the levels of these Magic Three hormones begin to rise erratically, abruptly, and dramatically. These increases, combined with major brain development, obvious outward changes in appearance, and the onset of smoldering teen angst are enough to put the volcanic activity of Vesuvius to shame. Welcome to the world of adolescence and the secret chemistry of desire. Approaching a teenage girl in the grip of the Magic Three is like approaching an electrical wire that has gone down in the wind and is flipping back and forth from the force of its own current. To make matters even more complicated, menstruation throughout the early and mid-teens is often irregular and can remain so for months and sometimes years. Although this irregularity is not abnormal, unpredictable bleeding, sometimes accompanied by severe cramping, abdominal bloating, and severe mood swings, is not uncommon, and these symptoms are difficult to manage physically and emotionally—for girls *and* their families. Our menses aren't called the curse without reason!

While not every girl is subject to extreme hormonally influenced highs and lows, all girls experience some degree of difficulty during this stabilization process. What's important to keep in mind about teenage girls is that their hormones have some influence on all aspects of their maturation and maturation occurs at a different rate for each girl.

When girls come in to my office for care, I always take advantage of the opportunity to educate them about how their bodies are changing and also about fertility and pregnancy. My experience has revealed that most of the time, teens have no idea of what their bodies are doing and why. My recent visit with Heather is a perfect example of this.

Heather was 14 and came to see me because her menstrual cramps were so bad she couldn't stand them. She also had developed "really bad headaches that make me puke sometimes." She was able to tell me that her periods started around age 12, that they only came once in awhile in the beginning, but that lately she was feeling like she had her period "all the time." She reported missing school at least one to three days every month because of her symptoms. She denied ever having been sexually active but said she wanted birth control pills because she had heard they can "help with the cramps and headaches." This was a reasonable request under the circumstances.

Before I actually gave her the prescription, I told her I wanted to make sure she understood what was happening that was making her feel so miserable and how the birth control pills worked to relieve her symptoms. When I added information about ovulation, being fertile when you ovulate, and the nuts-and-bolts basics of how girls get pregnant, it was like talking to a deer in the headlights. Clearly, I had just told Heather many things she had never heard before.

Young teens, between the ages of 13 and 15, who tell me they want birth control may have no intention of using it for contraception. These girls are simply looking for some relief from their menstrual misery. This is reasonable. These overwhelmingly popular pharmaceuticals are well known, even among the lay population of naïve teens, to improve the symptoms of PMS, decrease menstrual cramping, and grant their users a heads-up on when to stuff their purses and backpacks with feminine hygiene products. Very nice side effects for a tiny tablet originally developed to prevent pregnancy. Oh yes, and they do that too! The irony is that nearly all my teen patients—and many adults I see—have no idea why these pills are so effective in relieving women's monthly miseries and how that relates to why they're 98 percent effective in preventing pregnancy when taken as directed. Birth control pills work by overriding normal hormonal function and levels, thus interfering with the maturation and release of an egg, which is what ovulation is all about. When the release of the egg is interrupted by hormone pills, (i.e., birth control pills) girls and women are rendered infertile and, therefore, don't get pregnant.

Meanwhile, moving up from "down there," other physical changes are occurring in teenage girls that may affect how they feel about themselves and their bodies. Breast development—especially when it appears (as it often does) disproportionate to the rest of a girl's body—leaves everyone suffering from Pink Elephant in the Room syndrome. Family members will move around these breasts while not being able to take their eyes off them and definitely not mentioning them. Mothers are frantic; fathers are stunned and uncomfortable; and girls are left in a peculiar lurch. It's a combination of *Wow, how cool* and *Oh, my God! I hate these things.* Hormones are powerful things and the impact they have on girls' bodies is profound. When my own daughter was about 14 or so, her body was an impressive sight, breasts included. In what I believe was a semiconscious, half-baked effort to test the waters and see how others would respond to her budding womanhood, she decided to informally poll the residents of our small but popular town with a walk down Main Street in an outfit that was intended to show off her new—under the influence of hormones—figure.

As fashion ingénues, young teen girls can come out with some amazingly shocking outfits. Seemingly oblivious, young teens appear to lack a working knowledge of how simply bare their bodies can be at times and will choose to wear garments of the lowest thread count per inch no matter what the weather or the circumstances. Fashion choices are based on mood: sexy, very sexy, or too hot to touch. My daughter was no exception, and the consequences provided a fabulous learning opportunity. Sporting some insanely scanty clothing, my then 14-year-old girl strutted her stuff in our town. As luck would have it, her stepbrother, six years older and wiser and fabulously protective, was there too. Although Thalia actually missed it, a car full of teenage boys drove by and one yelled out the window to her: "Do you want to suck my cock?" Her brother reacted by flipping them the finger while his sister stood there, happily soaking up the attention without any idea of what had really happened. My stepson asked her if she had actually heard what was said and then, when it was clear she hadn't, repeated the comment with appropriate disdain. My daughter then asked: "Well, did they say it in a nice way?" This comment could only come from a 14-year-old who has lost her mind to the overwhelming sensations of her sexual energy in combination with her predominant naïveté. My dear stepson pointed out to her that there was no good way to say something like that and that her outfit was likely to elicit more of these undesirable comments. At his insistence, she walked home and changed into something more suitable and less provocative. Thank goodness for older siblings with more insight and common sense. My daughter was better able to hear this from her stepbrother than she ever would have been from me. I was grateful for the lesson he gave her.

Now, let's complicate matters further. While estrogen and progesterone are increasing and trying their darndest to do so with some cyclic regularity, testosterone, which we almost always forget women have, is simply going up and staying up, creating even more sexual desire in this already demanding, turbulent, and complicated scenario. What accompanies desire is the biologically fueled mandate to individuate (to become a distinct and separate individual), in part, by establishing intimate relationships with someone (or sometimes anyone) other than your parents. It's kind of like having Robert Goulet singing "I've got to be me, do it or die, I've got to be me" in your head 24/7. Being "me" translates into "I *must* separate from my parents," and the drive to do so can feel stronger than the girl herself. One of the ways girls establish this essential separation is by developing a loving relationship with a partner. Another way is just by finding somebody to have sex with. In either case, it's definitely *not* something that has anything directly to do with their parents and really is an experience that is all about them!

If mothers/parents slip into a fugue state, start dissociating, or are simply too pained or panicked—for whatever reasons—by what's happening to their girls to help them, the consequences are almost always negative.

Having sex with my boyfriend makes me feel like I'm not going to be like my parents. Sex is important to me and I like the ways it feels. My mother acts like this is the worst thing that I could be doing but I think it's great and my boyfriend and I like getting it on. It's my own private thing and none of my parents' business. It's fine with me if my mother doesn't want to talk to me about it because I don't want to talk to her about it either. Nobody I have sex with does IV drugs so I'm not gonna get HIV.
— Taylor, 14

In my role as a midwife, I see this every day in my practice. When I explain to girls and women exactly what their bodies are doing, what to expect at various times and from various systems throughout the month, how their feelings relate to their hormones and how best to increase their overall comfort, well-being and safety, my patients are attentive, and often fascinated and grateful. It's a bit like providing the Cliff Notes version of an owner's manual. Tracey, a 13-year-old girl brought to me by her caring and appropriate stepmother, was the perfect person to receive this sort of information.

Tracey had been the unfortunate victim of coerced intercourse which occurred with a 16-year-old boy she knew from school. The specifics of the circumstances surrounding this event were unclear but the primary objective of her visit with me was absolutely clear: rule out pregnancy, test for STIs, and educate this young teen about staying safe while screening for the possibility of continued sexual activity and the need for contraception. Sadly, this was her first experience with partnered sex. But fortunately she had a strong and open relationship with her stepmother (also my patient) who made an appointment for her to see me immediately.

Tracey was an immature 13-year-old girl, and it was easy to pick up on her vulnerability—as no doubt her coercive older partner had also done. My time gathering pertinent information as well as completing her exam involved a combination of monologue and dialogue: the anatomy of her vagina, what and where her cervix was and why I needed to access it to test for STIs, the relationship between her last period and her negative pregnancy test (phew!). I also asked her about the likelihood of her future interest in being sexually active—despite her disinterest at present—and discussed how she can keep herself safe from events like the one that brought her in to see me. This included talking with her about avoiding the use of alcohol and drugs, which can increase a girl's risk of sexual assault, by making her feel more sexual but leaving her less capable of warding off advances when unsolicited.

Tracey listened to everything I said and made eye contact with me whenever possible. Even her stepmother was listening, as if hearing this information for the first time—and perhaps she was. It is remarkable how many of us reach adulthood without even knowing the basics about our sexual biology.

The body is an amazing machine, and the medical establishment has a long history of keeping this information inaccessible and incomprehensible to the very people who need it most. More important, knowing the facts about how estrogen, progesterone, and testosterone affect your brain, your behaviors, and your body really does help girls and women make better decisions and choices in life. This is especially relevant when it comes to partnered sex.

Estrogen, progesterone, and testosterone aren't the only things affecting our daughters' behavior. Their brain hormones and brain function are factors as well.

Human beings have what is called a triune brain. Essentially, this means that we have three parts to our brains that all speak to one another while having distinctly separate functions. Understanding how each of these three brains work independently and together can help us all understand what is going on in a girl's mind during puberty.

The Inner Lizard

The back of our brain is known as the reptilian brain. Yup, just like lizards and frogs. Think of this part of your brain as the major control panel that operates the basic functions that keep you alive; and that's about it. The reptilian brain is the very thing that keeps you breathing when you are otherwise known as "brain dead." Those features and behaviors that make us undeniably human and *not* reptilian are dependent on the higher functioning areas of the brain known as the limbic brain and the neocortical brain.

THE LIMBIC BRAIN

Limbic brain function is more complex than that of the reptilian brain. It is highly sensitive, yet not particularly specific. In other words it's a very reactive part of the human brain, but not always clear and/or precise about what it's reacting to. Sound familiar? Well, it should because this is the part of the brain your teenage girl uses and relies on most.

The limbic brain is the control panel for the detection of threat, mammalian connection, and emotionality. At the heart of the limbic brain and its reactive nature is a small but powerful organ called the amygdala. This organ's primary function is the detection of threat, impending danger, or approaching harm. The amygdala directly connects to our sympathetic nervous system, which tells us to duck and take cover in the face of danger. Most of us know this as the fight-or-flight response. Thanks to the amygdala, we experience acceleration in our heart rate when the threat of danger is present, and relaxation once safety and security have been confirmed. The problem is, while the amygdala is highly sensitive, it's not capable of deciphering specific, and often very helpful, information about the perceived threat. This means that in many teens, who are usually limbic brain–dominated creatures, you may get the very same fight-or-flight response to saying "Please take out the garbage," as you would to saying, "By the way, the house is on fire." You tell your daughter that her skirt is too short and she wants to launch a revolution, as if you were depriving her of life, liberty, and the pursuit of happiness. When these inevitable flights of fury ensue, try to remember that it's not really your daughter talking, it's her limbic brain speaking on her behalf.

The Neocortical Brain

When the amygdala receives a danger signal, the signal is immediately transmitted to the neocortex for end-stage processing. The neocortex, also known as the frontal lobe, is the part of the brain that distinguishes us from other mammals. When fully developed, it allows us the use of language, executive processing, and even abstract conceptualization. In teenagers, the limbic brain is mature, but the neocortex is a comparative fledgling and simply can't yet do the job as well as we would like.

Further, in teens, there is lag time between the limbic brain picking up the signals and then transmitting them to the neocortex. This gives adolescents plenty of time for the sense of threat to fully sink in and for their behavior to reflect this, which is where the problems begin. This lag time is what results in the door slamming, the eye rolling, and the outlandish accusations. This is the exact place where world-class teen dramas are born. Asking teenagers to make their beds seems like an odd trigger for a tirade against family government. And asking your daughter to be home by eleven doesn't seem like it should warrant an impassioned speech on how you are murdering her soul. And yet, to a teenager in the throes of limbic response with an immature brain filter, this is exactly what it feels like. Throw in the limbic-based responses of tired and overworked parents, and it's no wonder that all hell can break loose. This is why the parents of teenagers must rely heavily on their fully developed and mature higher brain functions in such moments!

There is an upside to being limbic brain–centered creatures. Adults often spend a disproportionate amount of time problem-solving and thinking critically as they move through the world. This may be more interesting and captivating in many ways but it keeps us at a distance from how we feel about all sorts of things. It also keeps us at arm's length from our sexuality, which is highly limbic brain–centered.

Our teenage daughters reside much more so than we do in their highly sensitive limbic brains and as a consequence move through the world with a propensity for drama but also a predominant awareness of their emotions and sexuality. It's not that one part of the brain is actually superior to the other. We wouldn't be such complex and interesting beings without both. The key is achieving a balance between the two that will result in success for adults and teens. Under normal circumstances and simply through the passage of time, these areas of the teen brain mature and develop a harmonious and impressive relationship that allows for amazing creativity, comprehension, and accomplishment in a fully realized adult. So don't despair. Just like teething and toilet training, this developmental phase of life passes once our teenagers reach maturity. So try to remind yourself, it's just a phase.

Like the endocrine system, which directs and affects levels of estrogen, progesterone, and testosterone, the neurological system has its own group of specific chemical substances that affect teenage behavior. Dopamine, serotonin, and oxytocin, for example, all respond to both external and internal stimulus. These hormones are generally associated with positive, feel-good states, and rise in response to things humans enjoy like emotional connection, skin-to-skin contact, and/or sex, for example.[1] These experiences represent limbic brain resonance at its finest and most appreciated. When we experience this kind of connection, the "hum" that ensues is beautiful and deeply satisfying. Two people, enjoying each other's company, moving closer and closer until closeness becomes captivating, arousing physical fusion is one of the experiences that make it so great to be human.

If you're a teenager, your endocrine system is driving you to this behavior with ever increasing urgency, and once you're engaged in it, you get the ultimate payoff—you get sex stoned. When dopamine, serotonin, and oxytocin levels are nice and high, you experience the afterglow that people talk about. When the hormones of the endocrine system and the neurological system combine in one human being's experience of themselves and the world, it can keep them coming back for more and more, and then even more after that. This is the power of limbic brain resonance and attunement between two hormonally driven, willing sex partners, one of whom may be your teenage daughter.

It is nearly impossible for many parents to imagine that their teen girls are actually capable of lusting after another person with X-rated abandon. The idea that our baby girls could have the wanton sex drive of an alpha she-wolf in heat is more than we can bear. But our daughters are first and foremost human and, as a consequence, subject and slave to their bodies and their biological shifts. Like it or not—lust included.

Kurt came over Friday night. Things are going fairly well. When he was with me Friday night we had really good sex. He was extremely affectionate toward me and touched me the way I really like people to treat me when I'm in bed with them. We also talked a lot and I felt so close to him that I was able to tell him that I've never had an orgasm with anyone I've ever slept with. That's something I've never told anyone. He was really understanding and when I asked him to see if he could make me cum he told me he'd do anything for me and to tell him what I wanted. It was really weird because he had never been this way with me before.

— Elizabeth, 16

Parents who freak out over the mere thought that their daughters would engage in sex, never mind actually enjoy sex , end up adding a third chemical component to the mix: cortisol. The more upset and anxious one gets, the more cortisol they release, and the more cortisol that is released, the more confusion people experience. When the neocortex is flooded with large amounts of cortisol, the individual simply can't think straight and will really start to panic.[2] The worst thing about panic and anxiety is that they can be highly contagious, especially to a person whose amygdala is extremely sensitive to but not very discerning of highly emotive states. In this situation both mother and daughter are going to suffer, for the same and different reasons. Daughter *was* feeling good until mom found out about what made her feel that way. When mom wigs out, daughter wigs out even more and neither one makes much sense. It's everybody's nightmare!

If parents aren't able or willing to separate their values from the impact that biology has on their daughters' behavior, that's when we typically see parent-daughter relationships becoming (and staying) extremely complicated, distressing, and potentially destructive for kids.

Watching our daughters turn into young women right before our eyes is startling at the very least. Further, the changes often happen in fits and starts so while seemingly dormant at any given moment, suddenly two weeks later undeniable, huge changes are noticeable. It's stressful to live with this much sudden and sweeping change, and it can become difficult for parents and daughters to feel as if they know the identity of the person they're talking to. One moment your daughter is looking and acting like the innocent and agreeable ten-year-old you knew well and remember best. At other moments, she looks like she should be strutting down a catwalk in Milan before dashing off for cocktails with a photographer, and she's late so get out of her way already! Girls notice these disparate states too.

Growing up is somewhat of an impossible thing to do. Maybe it's not growing up that's so difficult. Maybe it's just me not being the me that I was used to.

— Victoria, 17

Regardless of whether they say yes or no to sex with a partner, parents of teens are doing the right thing by acknowledging the existence and normalcy of their sexual interests and feelings. Your bringing up the subject will not be suggestive, nor will it be what triggers your daughter's sexual awakening and desire.

PLANTING THE SEEDS OF PLEASURE

Somehow the idea of sexuality for sheer pleasure is persistently underdiscussed with teen girls, if it's mentioned at all. The focus that parents have on the potential hazards and risks of sex presents a skewed version of the real point of having sex in the first place, and can give our girls the idea that sex is a bad and dangerous thing. This message can affect their sexual health and satisfaction negatively for the rest of their lives, as it has for many mothers when they were teenage daughters themselves.

Telling girls that sex should feel good is, frankly, a radical idea. And if we think we're putting them in harm's way by "giving them ideas," this is simply wrong. Here's where the brain steps in again. The idea that touch feels good has already been well established by you, their loving and attentive mothers. After all the years that you have soothed, caressed, stroked and held your little girl, she is perfectly acquainted with the feel-good aspects of being touched by someone who is attentive and loving toward her. So what exactly is wrong with making her aware that being touched in the context of a loving sexual partnership is a pleasurable and healthy part of life?

If the fear in parents stems from worries that girls will make bad choices by acting on their sexual impulses, then parents must be willing to beef up the information and support they provide their daughters as sexual beginners so their daughters will be more likely to make informed choices, thus lessening their risks for disaster. Helping girls negotiate these feelings by acknowledging them in the first place is the most important step to take. This is not synonymous with giving our daughters tacit approval for acting on these impulses and engaging in partnered sex. There are alternatives like fantasizing and reading about sex and developing a guilt-free masturbatory practice. But the important element is to stress sex as a positive and natural part of development, not a scourge to be avoided at all costs, even in conversation!

Nature has chosen this time in their lives to exert powerful forces on our daughters' bodies, brains, and psychology; and there is no going back. It is one of the times in human development when biology and behavior are inextricably linked and when hormones fuel longings and impulses, whether anyone likes it or not. Erratic and absolute increases in levels of the Magic Three during adolescence affect teens and parents like a tidal wave. Parents feel overwhelmed, completely unprepared, and desperate for the storm to pass. Teens, on the other hand, experience some pleasure and enjoyment as the wave barrels through and the water rises, especially when it comes to their sexuality.

Contrary to popular opinion, however, teen lust and the sex that may ensue are not the enemies for parents to go up against. Instead, it's uninformed and unmentored sex—the kind that many of our kids are having—that we need to vanquish. Believe it or not, this is a manageable foe and parents are the best people to go head to head with it. You know your kids best.

QUESTIONS TO ASK YOURSELF

Before you go on to the next chapter, ask yourself the following questions and refer back to them as often as necessary as you read this book. They will help you clarify what you really want for your daughter and how achieving this is likely to be more possible than you might think.

- What are you most afraid of when you think about your daughter developing sexually?

- Can you recall your own experiences with and feelings about sex as a teen? Do you want these to be the same or different for your daughter?

- What have you done to normalize sex in conversations, both with your daughter and in your own life?

- What is your optimal goal when it comes to your daughter's emerging sexuality?

- How do you want your daughter to feel about and treat her developing body?

CHAPTER 2

THE UNSPOKEN MEAN
OF TEEN BODY-SPEAK

"I speak two languages: Body and English."

— Mae West

Parenting your daughter through adolescence demands a tremendous amount of stamina, a willingness to read between the lines, and the ability to interpret her body language. Sometimes, teens simply lack the ability to articulate what they feel. At these times, teenagers often use their bodies like billboards to display their feelings, new and growing body parts, and their ever-expanding sense of self. This is what I call teen body-speak, which is made up of three primary components; body image, fashion sense, and health awareness. All are independent yet interconnected. And all will be used to exhibit the work-in-progress of your daughter's emerging young adult self.

The three things mothers tend to comment on or criticize most about their girls are specific to their bodies: hair, clothing, and weight.[1] However, attention is best paid from a distance and comments are most useful if kept to a minimum. They should be objective and relative to your daughter's own opinions. This will allow your teenager plenty of room for experimentation while continuing to have you close by, just in case she needs you.

Your daughter's adolescence provides you with opportunities to positively influence her relationship with and to her body as well as her sexuality and sexual expression. It's been my experience that mothers have much more influence over their daughters than they realize. Exerting it wisely helps to insure their daughters' future sexual and emotional health.

Media perpetuation of unreal images of girls and women, mother's ideas and values about physical beauty, peer opinions, and the emphasis on appearance in publications geared toward teens all find a common dumping ground in the laps of teenage girls. Look at any magazine for teen girls and you'll see that at least 30 percent of the content focuses on the importance of being pretty. In addition, half of these magazines use the idea of beauty to promote the sale of products.[2] This exacerbates and underscores one of the most trying and difficult aspects of being a teenager: feeling conspicuous under all circumstances and to everyone—especially themselves.

Changes in physical appearance, as the child's body becomes the teen's body, introduce girls to the experience and responsibility of managing objectification at a particularly vulnerable time in their development. Girls are constantly pulled into states of conspicuousness because their bodies are changing so radically. It's difficult for them to keep pace with the rate of change and the reactions they incite. Now, with new bodies that everyone seems to be noticing and hormonal changes that render them sexually charged, girls begin sliding down that slippery slope of preoccupation with appearance. This is the time that obsessive thinking about being "pretty enough" takes hold and for some girls never leaves them in peace. A mother's choice of words and actions, at this time especially, makes a big difference in how her daughter will feel about herself for the rest of her life.

Just as soon as I think I have become who I am going to be as an adult, I noticed that my pants weren't buttoning easily anymore and my hips seemed wider. Then my skin broke out—literally overnight! Not only that, but my bras became too small and I started to feel like I had the biggest boobs in my class—without question. Between feeling fat, having zits, and growing gigantic tits all at once, I felt like I never wanted to come out of my room again.
— Emily, 14

Almost without exception there is a crucial connection between a teen's body image and that of her mother. This is a double-edged sword, because while it's encouraging to know that mothers can significantly influence the development of a positive body image in their daughters, mothers must realize they can also contribute to the development of a dangerously negative body image.

Mothers who regularly stand in front of a full-length mirror and degrade themselves for everything from excess weight to normal signs of aging plant the seeds for similar, if not identical, monologues and behaviors in their daughters. This negative talk happens in other places too, like the dinner table, while exercising (or not), while getting dressed, or while shopping for clothes. Although we may assume that our comments about ourselves fall on deaf ears, our daughters actually listen quite closely. What we are saying to ourselves about ourselves can have long-lasting effects on our daughters' developing body image and sexuality.

In my own life as a full-figured gal (since the age of two) I reaped the benefits of a mother whose commentaries on appearance—hers, mine, and others—served me well through adolescence and continue to do so now in middle age. My Greek mother is petite, slim, and very pretty: the opposite of me. Although our faces are a bit similar and I was fortunate to inherit her beautiful eye color, our bodies couldn't be more different. At five foot three my mother never weighed more than 115 pounds. I reached this weight by fourth grade. I inherited my Czechoslovakian father's body, with broad shoulders and plenty of lean muscle mass mixed in with the fat, and my paternal grandmother's ample bosom. I was a strong and cherished farm animal in my family and everyone spotted my strength early on, assigning me all sorts of chores unusual for my age—"get Evie to move that chair, she's really strong"—never mind that I was seven. Meanwhile, I cannot remember a time when my mother criticized my body in such a way that I felt terrible about how I looked. My mom's soapbox was all about elegance, style, and manners. If you didn't measure up to her standards, then look out! You'd have to do plenty to get back in her graces. But as for me, she never told me that my body size, shape, or fat were hopeless or mortal flaws. And when others did, she was my greatest advocate. (She even went to the extent of suggesting I punch someone "really hard" in grade school who was persisting in calling me hurtful names. I did and she was very pleased.) She also never complained about how she looked. And, unlike virtually every other woman we knew, she refused to conceal or lie about her age. At a time when women weren't waiting as long to have babies as my mid-30s mother had, she would announce her age with gusto and shame others who wouldn't do the same.

By the time I was raising my own daughter, I decided I needed to take the same approach my mother had and leave the commentaries alone. Ultimately, it didn't matter what my daughter looked like; I would love her anyway, as my mother had loved me. As history is known to do, it repeated itself in the next generation: my daughter and I look nothing alike. Our only shared features are our voice pattern and our noses. She is an intercontinental beauty who turns heads wherever she is in the world and has done so since she was born. My daughter's lean and lovely figure and beautiful face have resulted in our family's favorite joke of all: "That's *your* daughter?" The parenthetical digression being: "How could this have possibly happened? She looks *nothing* like you!"

Raising a beautiful daughter and not sharing her beauty made me work with particular diligence to avoid overemphasizing my own shock over the peculiarities of genetics and the facts of her physical beauty. Instead, I focused on the state of my health and hers. While everyone else we encountered felt entitled to point out the dramatic contrast between the two of us, I continued to plod along (strong farm animal that I am) and, like my mother, focus on elegance and style as far more important than beauty. Meanwhile, I did and continue to have occasional struggles with the kind of physical beauty that has eluded me and which has been granted to both my first-degree relatives. I am convinced that what saved me from despair and the life of a social recluse or chronic plastic surgery junkie has been my focus on health and humor as more important attributes, and both have served me well. They have rubbed off on my daughter, too.

When Thalia was in her mid-teens, she ran into my room with a sense of urgency to report something in the way only adolescent girls can. I was half-dressed and evidently the sight of my ample and aging breasts knocked the wind right out of her. It also made her very pale. Thinking she was having an acute asthma attack, I asked her if she was okay. Her reply had nothing to do with her respiratory status. She looked at me with the greatest concern and sincerity and asked, "Are *those* in my future?" As a mother I had a decision to make about which route to take at that moment. Should I respond with embarrassment and equal dismay, or was there humor to be found in this moment? I opted for the latter: I cupped my breasts in my hands, hoisted them up, and, like the best of the 1940s pinup girls, turned to the side, looked coyly at her, and said, "Do you mean these enviable beauties?" At this point my daughter relaxed and, being as good humored as I am, started to laugh. I then told her, in no uncertain terms, that these breasts were not to be feared and, in fact, had been her lifeblood and favorite things for the two and a half years that she nursed. I also emphasized the health and wellness that her superior food source had granted her and that this undoubtedly had something to do with her loveliness and strong constitution.

I look on this moment as my way of doing the best I could do for my daughter in the same way my mother had done for me. No need nor benefit in criticizing myself at both our expense.

In a 2006 study by the Girl Scout Research Institute, 3,000 girls ages 11–17 from varied socioeconomic and racial backgrounds identified their mother's behaviors and comments as significantly contributing to their feelings about their bodies and appearance, including their sense of satisfaction with their weight.[3]

The girls I see in my midwifery practice who express confidence in their bodies and appearance are often physically fit, maintain healthy eating habits, nonsmoking, and rarely have a sexual abuse history. These girls also have mothers with similar behaviors and history. Many of them are sexually active with one partner, male or female, and are at low risk for developing problems related to their sexuality. Generally speaking, they like their bodies and what they are able to experience in them, whether it's sports or sex. They live without the constant voice of criticism that is part of so many of their peers' lives.

The number of girls who struggle with the perceptions of themselves, particularly when it comes to weight and body size, has been growing. These girls often end up with serious health problems. For this reason, the topic of girls' eating habits and weight have become well-warranted concerns among health care practitioners, parents, and educators.

No matter what I do and who I am, I just don't feel like I'll ever stand a chance to have someone like me if I am not thin. The boys at my school all want thin girls. Nobody likes a fat girl. I

think the best looking girls are the ones that are the thinnest—
that is why I always watch what I eat. This is what you see in
fashion magazines, too. You never see fat models.

— Tanya, 15

The Dangers of Trying to Be Picture Perfect

Beauty and style, as portrayed by mass media, present an especially complicated and influential force for teen girls and their parents to interpret and counter. In this era of photo retouching and magical special effects, the pictures of girls and women in magazines, on billboards, and in newspapers are so altered that they barely resemble what they look like in real life. Fabricated, adjusted, and tweaked to fit an impossible ideal, the girls and women we see who are selling products geared toward other women in their age group are utterly and completely false: no cellulite, no gravitational effect on breasts, no split ends, unblemished skin, and impossibly perfect teeth.

With the exception of the Dove Campaign for Real Beauty, which is specifically designed to combat the assault on women's body image by the media, no other companies in the cosmetic or women's clothing industries have so openly or directly addressed the falsehoods in today's advertising. In fact, few companies have actually taken the initiative to include the regular, perhaps fuller-figured, non–runway model body type in their advertising. Until the emergence of plus-size model Emme there had been few examples of physically fit, beautiful, full-figured women selling cosmetics or clothes. Short of a moratorium on all publications, television, videos, and movies, we simply can't keep this stuff away from our girls. But we can openly call it what it is—artificial and unreal—and we can make sure that we as moms aren't buying into these unreal media definitions of beauty when it comes to ourselves and the way we address our own mirror.

I feel fat all the time, and I know I look fat, no matter what I eat. I hate my body because of it, and even though my parents tell me that I look fine, I know they talk about how I look all the time—they always have, especially my mother. She has talked to me about dieting since I was in second grade, and I have dieted ever since grade school.
— Elaine, 14

Negative looking-glass reflections and articulated critiques perpetuate one of the most dangerous cultural myths women face: that there is such a thing as perfect beauty, and if you just shop, diet, use a certain beauty product, or have the right surgery, you'll eventually achieve it. Further, the encoded belief that perfect beauty leads to romance, sex, and love makes for a particularly addictive potion which is frequently administered in large doses throughout the teen years. This is dangerous business when you're working with a body and mind that are under construction and particularly susceptible to errors in wiring. As many adult women will attest, trying to amend the mistake after the walls are up and the building is complete is a costly, lengthy, and arduous task.

Unquestionably, I have days when I sadly fantasize about what I have never been and will never be—slim, a stunner, taller than five foot five, and well known to all because of my physical beauty. By my late teens I realized that the way to manage whatever disappointments I might have about my figure was to capitalize on my physical strength. This was when I became a competitive power-lifter, squatting 260 pounds at my last competition when I was 22. It was a fabulous experience to walk out, weighing over 190 pounds, in front of a room full of strangers who had come to see what the big girls could do. And I was one of those big girls. I have a photograph of this moment in my office, and I glance at it regularly—for inspiration and a reminder that big isn't bad, but weak will get you nowhere.

Taking advantage of the positive aspects of your body will take you a long way. Humor is a woman's second best defense against despair—this is especially true when we find ourselves up against deeply upsetting feelings about our own sense of inadequacy or imperfection. Humor defuses anxiety, is relaxing, and if practiced often enough becomes infectious. It is an important coping skill that can be used at any time. Believe it or not, there is something funny to be said about everything, and laughter is strong and effective medicine. It provides not only great emotional immunity to despair but also a powerful remedy when the despair takes hold. When we remain actively upset and can't diffuse or extinguish our feelings with humor or physical pleasure, the deleterious effects are intense and our negative feelings about ourselves can affect every aspect of our sense of self.

I had just returned from my pool workout during lunch when Rhonda came to see me for a routine annual gynecological exam. She was 25, and I noted from her chart that she hadn't seen anyone for care in a couple of years. When I walked into the room, I saw a very heavy-set woman whose disposition was notably withdrawn. Rhonda's weight was blank in her chart, but by my best estimate she was well over 200 pounds and was approximately five foot three.

Rhonda told me that she had had a significant change in her period and was bleeding heavily and often. She was worried about what this might mean. She remarked on the length of time since her last visit. When I asked her more about this, she told me that she had gained at least 50 pounds over the last couple of years and that although she had always struggled with being overweight, she had never been as heavy as she was now. She said she had been too embarrassed about her body to come in for care and added that she was relieved I was a heavyset woman also, as this made her feel more comfortable. Once my exam was over and we agreed on a plan to manage her bleeding, I started a conversation with her about her weight and expressed my concerns about her general health and the direction in which her weight had gone.

Rhonda told me a common story. She had always been a "fat kid" and was teased at school. She was also frequently criticized by her mother who repeatedly made her feel bad about her weight. Her mother was lean and very fearful of getting fat, fearing that everything that she ate had the potential for making her fat. She never exercised regularly but would go through periods of short-lived diet and exercise programs that were impossible to sustain, unhealthy and very influential on Rhonda. Worst of all, Rhonda reported feeling more loved by her mother when she was thinner! (Sadly, I have heard this from many women like Rhonda.) I realized at 25 Rhonda had experienced a lifetime of self-hatred that I wasn't going to change in one visit. But I began a conversation with her that she had never heard before.

I explained to her that whatever she weighed was less important to me in terms of her health than if she exercised regularly and often. I advised her to stop thinking about the number on the scale and instead focus on increasing her activity level slowly and steadily by walking six days per week, starting with 30 minutes and building up slowly to an hour each day. In addition, I suggested she employ the "hot potato" method to the negative thoughts she had about her body. In other words, every time she heard a negative voice inside her head saying something mean about her body, she should drop the thought like a hot potato and replace it with something positive—about anything—be it weather, her intelligence, or her favorite pet. Anything positive would work. The objective was to reduce the number of negative thoughts that she kept company with every day. I also suggested that she had heard enough from her mother about her weight. I suggested she tell her mother that she wasn't allowed to comment anymore about her body or what she ate. Saying this was a prescription for her and part of my plan. I asked her to come back and see me for a follow-up visit in three months and at that point, we'd evaluate my interventions for her bleeding. This future visit would also give me a chance to see how she was doing with my other suggestions. Before she left, I managed to get her to make a commitment to me to try what I had suggested, and she agreed.

Three months later, she kept her appointment and had kept her promise to exercise regularly and was working to stop the self-deprecating chatter using the hot potato method. Things weren't perfect, but they were better. She looked better, felt better, and although she still struggled, her burden was lessened. She also had mustered the courage to tell her mother to stop making comments about her body, and amazingly, she hadn't heard anything since. Rhonda was on the road to improved health, and she sensed the difference. This was a huge first step in changing her lifelong negative body image and improving her health. She even cracked a joke on that second visit—this was real progress!

Taking an Honest Look at Your Teen

It's easier than you might realize to assess whether the media or stringent rules about eating and exercise imposed by self or family are affecting your daughter's health. Take a serious look at her and be honest with yourself about what you see.

Watch when and what your girl is eating, and listen to her comments about food and what she is saying to herself and others about her body. When you pay attention to the formation of your daughter's body image, you gain valuable information about her general health and her feelings about how her body looks. If you start to notice that your daughter rarely eats in front of you, is looking sallow, wears clothes too big for her, exercises excessively, complains of being too fat all the time, has stopped having her period, or has frequent diarrhea or constipation, you're probably seeing signs of an eating or exercise disorder. If this is the case, expressing your concerns directly and persistently is crucial for your daughter to get the help she needs. Further, be honest with yourself about your own behaviors and look for similarities between yours and hers.

In contrast, if she's being asphyxiated by her jeans, has made it clear that soda is her beverage of choice, loves fast food, and never moves from the computer screen except to go to the bathroom, this situation requires your attention and intervention. In either case, the behaviors reflect a potentially poor or distant relationship with her body that can readily affect her self-image, sexual development, and overall emotional and physical health.

EATING DISORDERS

According to the Eating Disorders Coalition, the number of new cases of eating disorders in teens and young adults has doubled since 1960, and over 90 percent of people diagnosed are adolescents and young women.[4]

When pop star Karen Carpenter died in 1983 from anorexia, the reality that something terribly dangerous could and was happening to girls became newsworthy and a more common topic of discussion among parents and teens. Since then, ongoing research on eating disorders has yielded particularly troubling findings.

Eating disorders affect all segments of society, crossing socioeconomic and racial lines. Because 86 percent of all those affected report onset of their illness by the age of 20, awareness of the types of disorders that occur, their symptoms, and their consequences is an important part of parenting an adolescent girl.[5] Anorexia nervosa, bulimia, and obesity are the most common eating disorders. Each has specific characteristics, features, and symptoms, and yet they all have one thing in common: those suffering from these disorders have intense and extreme feelings and behaviors associated with food, eating, weight, and body image. Many women will wrestle with these issues for the rest of their lives unless the situation is addressed as soon as it appears in adolescence. When undetected and untreated, these feelings and behaviors pose significant risks to a girl's physical and emotional health.

Anorexia Nervosa

Though *anorexia* means a loss of appetite, a girl with this condition doesn't actually lose her appetite but instead does everything she can to control it. She becomes obsessed with food and is constantly thinking about what she has and has not eaten. This obsessive thinking is driven by an underlying fear that everything she eats puts her at extreme risk for becoming fat. In addition, she develops an inaccurate perception of how her body looks and often complains about being fat when she is normal weight or even well below normal weight.

Refusal to maintain a normal weight, even when the dangers of extreme thinness are explained, is a key factor in diagnosis. Other symptoms include excessive focus on the number of calories in food as well as the number of calories being consumed, an intense fear of gaining weight, repeatedly reporting a lack of appetite (regardless of what has actually been consumed), thinning of hair or hair loss, abnormal weight loss, cessation of menstruation for three consecutive months or more, an increase in facial and body hair, sallow complexion, and osteoporosis.[6]

Causes of anorexia nervosa are not completely understood. Some researchers claim that there is a genetic link—that eating disorders are passed down from parents to their children. But this theory is relatively new and hasn't been well researched. Because of the increased prevalence of anorexia among girls, the relationships and environments that are most influential in girls' lives have been investigated most and the results are important to parents of girls, especially mothers.

Having a mother who is focused on thinness as a cornerstone for beauty and self-acceptance and who also obsesses about everything she eats gives a teen girl the message that food is to be feared, closely monitored, and always restricted. The idea of food as an undeniable source of fuel, pleasure, comfort, and celebration of community with others is lost among the frequent and constant negative comments. In combination with the self-deprecating and mean comments many women make about their appearances (and sometimes their daughters'), it's easy to imagine how anorexia can take hold and snowball into a dangerous and potentially life-threatening condition.

Not everyone whose mother is hyperattentive and conscious about food will develop anorexia, but teen girls do develop (and retain) all sorts of other unhealthy behaviors associated with food and eating that are dysfunctional and cause health problems.

Mary, an 18-year-old freshman in college, came to see me on her school vacation with a complaint of irregular periods and cramping that was occurring all month long, not just when she had her period. She also complained about not having much energy and that she was frequently tired, which was making it difficult to keep up with her studies. As is often the case when any unusual or problematic physical symptoms occur, girls and women assume there's something wrong with their hormones. This was Mary's assumption too.

Mary's abdominal exam revealed some tenderness and fullness, especially in the lower left side. Pelvic exam findings were normal. She was slightly below average weight, wasn't pregnant, rarely sexually active, and swore she used a condom every time she had intercourse. When I asked her to be more specific about her periods, she told me they came monthly, but were unpredictable and lasted between two and five days. This was essentially normal. I then asked her about her cramps and she said they occurred "all the time" and she had no idea what was causing them. In girl-speak, cramps mean menstrual cramps. But what girls and women forget is that there's more in our pelvises than our reproductive organs. Our uterus, fallopian tubes, and ovaries share space with our bowels and, generally speaking, if abdominal cramps aren't gynecologic in origin, they're likely to be related to bowel activity and diet. Suspecting this, I asked her questions about what and how she ate.

Mary told me she was a picky eater. This translated into no breakfasts, pizza for lunch, and maybe a yogurt, cottage cheese, or toast for dinner. If her dining hall at school didn't have what she wanted, she skipped the meal entirely. This meant that there were days when she wouldn't eat at all. When I asked her about vegetables and fruits, she said she didn't really like them—even though she was a vegetarian for health reasons. Based on her report, I estimated that Mary was eating between 800 and 1000 calories at most on the days she ate and then of course none on the days she didn't. She didn't exercise and drank "tons" of water. I then asked her about bowel activity, and she told me that she "went to the bathroom about once or twice a week." No wonder she had persistent cramps.

I told Mary that without a doubt her cramping was coming from her infrequent bowel movements and wasn't at all related to her period. She was constipated and this accounted for the fullness in her lower abdomen and her infrequent bowel movements, both of which were likely the result of her terrible diet. I also explained to her that her fatigue was due to the fact that she wasn't eating enough calories on a regular basis to keep up with the demands of her life. It was also why she wasn't moving her bowel more than twice weekly. By the look on her face, I might as well have been speaking Martian. The more I told her, the more apparent it became that she didn't have a clue what I was talking about.

Mary had grown up with a mother who would repeatedly mention how relieved she was that no one in their family was fat and that being overweight was the number one indicator of poor health—according to her. As a consequence, whatever it took to stay slim was all right by her, and while weight loss diets and exercise weren't ever really discussed, there was also no mention that food is the fuel that bodies need for adequate energy and regularity of function. As far as Mary's mother was concerned, everyone in the family was healthy because they weren't fat. Not being fat was the sole criteria for health. So if you're slim, you're all set.

The end result of our visit was a list of recommendations based on common-sense practices known for years to constitute a sound and healthy diet. They included a multi-vitamin daily; eating three meals each day; and fruits and vegetables with each meal, adding beans, nuts, and eggs to her diet for adequate protein since she didn't eat meat. I also advised her to include healthy fats from walnuts, avocados, and olive oil to aid in a multitude of bodily functions and to eat carbohydrates from whole grains for lasting energy. Last, I suggested she read an excellent book by Walter Willet titled *Eat, Drink, and be Healthy* to improve her understanding of why diet is so important to overall health. When I was done with my recommendations, her first question was whether or not she'd get fat if she ate the way I was suggesting. Oh dear, we had a long way to go!

Mary provides a perfect example of how "apples don't fall far from trees." This daughter was modeling her mother's behavior and she was paying a price for doing so. She was chronically constipated and had very limited energy. Although she wasn't anorexic and didn't have a diagnosable eating disorder, she did have disordered and dysfunctional eating. She had a poor relationship with food and it was affecting her health.

An article that appeared in the *Journal of Abnormal Psychology* noted that "eating disorders may be learned, at least partially, through the daughters modeling the mother's behavior."[7] Certainly in Mary's case this was true. Her eating problems were interfering with her success in school and her physical well-being.

Everyone tells me I am too thin, but I just think I am really healthy. There are so many girls in my school that are so fat and I don't want to be fat at all and it takes a lot of work not to be. I exercise every day for a couple of hours and am really careful about what I eat. I do weigh myself every day— sometimes a couple of times a day—just to be sure I'm not gaining any weight but I really think I'm fine. I've read that a lot of teenage girls don't have regular periods so I don't think it's so abnormal that I don't get one.

— Heather, 14

Bulimia

Bulimia is characterized by cycles of bingeing on foods followed by episodes of purging. The most important emotion associated with bulimia is the feeling that one cannot stop oneself or control the bingeing. Purging can manifest as self-induced vomiting or through the use of laxatives, enemas, or diuretics. Avoiding foods altogether for periods of time before starting the process over again is also common.

Unlike those with anorexia nervosa, girls with bulimia often maintain normal weight or can be overweight, making it more difficult to identify the presence of an eating disorder. However, as with anorexia, certain behaviors and symptoms are hallmarks of the disorder and associated with a degree of emotional distress that the sufferer feels unable to manage in a healthy way.

Immediate post-meal bathroom visits (to vomit), vacillating between eating normally or not eating at all to gross overconsumption, and degradation of dental health are important indicators of the presence of bulimia. In severe cases, esophageal bleeding and stomach rupture can result, causing serious damage to the digestive track or even death.

The persistence or frequency of bulimic purging has been linked to dysfunctional family relationships, sexual abuse, difficulty with mood regulation, depression, and addiction or substance abuse. Increased impulsivity has also been cited as a factor. In all instances, the bulimic is an individual who feels that she cannot control her behavior and that her behavior is controlling her.[8]

The role that mothers play in girls' developing bulimia isn't as clear as it is in anorexia. But often the influence of dysfunctional family relationships is involved, and bulimia sometimes coexists with other eating disorders, including anorexia. In addition, the poor relationship with the body that both anorexics and bulimics display, as well as their distorted body images, does relate to the kinds of behavior displayed by important adults, especially their family members, in girls' lives. This includes having parents with addiction and depression, which increases the risk for both in their children.

Obesity

Overeating that leads to obesity is a type of eating disorder now affecting one third of all kids in the U.S. The American Academy of Pediatrics has identified obesity as a major health problem facing young people. Following close behind is the dramatic rise in the number of pediatric patients who are being diagnosed with type II diabetes, which is a directly related consequence.[9] While much easier to diagnose and identify, obesity poses as many potential health hazards as anorexia and bulimia, although the onset of these risks may not be as acute as they are in anorexia and bulimia.

Obesity goes beyond being plump and is different than having "baby fat." Girls between the ages of 9 and 11 often develop fullness in their abdomens and buttocks as they begin to change shape and develop more womanly features. However, this increase in regional body fat disappears once their periods begin and their bodies continue developing. When pubertal girls don't shed these extra pounds or they add excessive and unnecessary fat to their frame, then they're at risk for becoming obese and staying obese throughout their adult lives, generally adding more weight with advancing age.

Joanie was a 23-year-old girl who had her first baby a few months before her appointment. She came into to see me for a refill on her birth control pills and brought her baby with her. I remembered her well from her pregnancy as she had developed gestational diabetes while she was pregnant. Gestational diabetes is not rare and its risks during pregnancy can be high to the baby and mother, so as a precaution all pregnant women are screened for it. Anyone can develop this complication but women with a family history of diabetes and obesity and those who begin the pregnancy overweight are at higher risk. In addition, while the condition usually resolves once a woman has delivered, developing it during pregnancy indicates an increased risk for becoming diabetic later in adult life. Because of this, Joanie and I had many discussions about good nutrition, normal weight gain in pregnancy, and sensible food choices.

Joanie's baby was now eight months old and very plump. She had been bottle-fed and was now starting to eat solid foods other than cereal. She was a darling infant—and an obese one. Her mother had gained more weight than was healthy in pregnancy and had lost little of it since delivery. Although she was no longer diabetic, Joanie clearly still needed diet and exercise counseling. Because we had a good rapport, I took advantage of our time and relationship and started a conversation with her about her eating habits and her super-sized baby, whom she clearly loved dearly.

Joanie had been heavy all her life and came from a family of obese parents and siblings. Her parents were in their early 50s and already experiencing the impact of chronic illnesses related to being overweight. Her father was diagnosed with type II diabetes at age 47, needed insulin, and took other medications for high blood pressure. After Joanie gave birth, her appreciative and generous family showered the midwives and nursing staff with enough candy to last until Halloween—which was six months away.

Given the size of Joanie's baby, her lack of weight loss since delivery, and her family history, I told Joanie we needed to talk about her weight and her baby's weight. I started by expressing my concern about both and asked her to tell me what she ate on a daily basis. It is often the case with overweight people that they have no real idea of how much they overeat so when they describe their intake, those of us in the know look for evidence of this. They also often miss or forget about the calories in beverages—juice especially. From Joanie's report, it was evident that she was unaware of how many calories she was actually eating and drinking daily. I explained that I was particularly concerned about how her eating habits and family tendency toward obesity were affecting her, and that they would likely be an issue for her daughter also if she didn't take hold of the situation now. Given her baby's appearance, the problem had already begun.

Joanie described her baby's diet and daily intake and I quickly saw what was happening: her concepts of normal quantities were being transferred to her baby so she was feeding her much more than she needed to eat. When I realized this, I referred her to the side panel of infant cereal to follow the recommendations on quantity, even though I knew it probably wouldn't seem like enough to her. I also told her not to worry that her baby wasn't getting enough if she didn't finish all her food at every meal or wasn't in the mood to eat it all sometimes, assuming she wasn't ill. Last, I suggested limiting the number of teething biscuits and cookies, regardless of her teething status. One teething biscuit a couple times a day was plenty. Several was adding too many calories to her diet.

I then switched to Joanie herself and was compassionate but honest and direct. I made it clear that if she didn't make serious changes in her diet and exercise habits, she was likely to continue gaining weight and develop obesity-related illnesses, as had her parents. I reminded her about the relationship between gestational diabetes and developing diabetes later in life. Joanie is intelligent and trusted me as her practitioner so she listened closely. She finally admitted she had been struggling and didn't really know what to do. I made basic suggestions to start with: become informed about portion size, stop drinking calories in juice and soda, eliminate high-calorie animal fats like butter, and stop eating altogether after 7:00 P.M. I also encouraged her to start walking daily for at least 30 minutes. This was plenty to begin with and would mean significant changes for her. As I often do, I scheduled a visit with her in three months to see how she was faring and to offer more support and guidance. People can't accomplish such changes without help.

The signs and symptoms of obesity are easy to identify: in a nutshell, increasing body size with accompanying decreases in physical activity. The formula is rather simple: too much food and too few calories burned. If you notice that your girl's body is getting bigger, her clothes are getting tighter, she's eating more than usual at meals, consuming snacks in large amounts, and isn't physically active on her own or in organized sports, then she's probably developing a problem with obesity right before your eyes.

Sometimes in families where everyone is heavyset and overweight, it's difficult to objectively view your daughter's size. In those cases, many parents just feel their girl is taking after them—and this is a problem. But this may be the point where a mother can become aware of how her own behavior is influencing her daughter's.

As with mothers of girls with anorexia, the behaviors of adult women who are overweight are just as important in shaping their daughters' behaviors and attitudes about health, food, and exercise. If you're a woman who never exercises, overeats daily, is beginning to have obesity-related health problems like high blood pressure, elevated cholesterol, diabetes, and impaired mobility, it's time to take a serious look at your own behaviors and body and the messages they convey to your girl. This is difficult to do but absolutely imperative for the sake of your health and your daughter's too.

Next to quitting smoking, weight loss and weight management—especially if you have the genes that persistently direct you to the plus-size department—are about the hardest things to do. You can live without cigarettes, alcohol, and daily lattes, but you can't live without food. When co-workers bring boxes of donuts into the office it's difficult to say "no thank you" when your real impulse is to grab the custard-filled one out of your co-worker's hand because she got to it before you did. To make matters worse, even though the food you eat may be killing you, it's perfectly legal. No one goes to jail for buying Krispy Kremes on the corner and then pedaling them to you in the office. Regardless of your age, weight, health status, or income, you can go to any store, buy whatever you want, whenever you want, and no one stops you.

I am well acquainted with the struggles of maintaining a reasonable weight and good health. Maintaining a healthy relationship with food and exercise has been a lifelong effort for me, especially as I age. As a friend in her mid-50s said to me once, "This is my body on food, and I have my genes to thank for it." My pal exercises regularly, eats conscientiously, and wears a size 14. For years she was very slim but only because she managed her diet the way many women do—she ate very little and exercised all the time. She also considered herself healthy because she wasn't fat. Eventually, she realized she wasn't healthy, even though she was thin. Just like my freshman patient who felt tired and was constipated all the time, my friend never felt as good she wanted to. Furthermore, she obsessed about food constantly in order to stay thin. When she came to terms with her genetic predisposition to be a size 14 and familiarized herself with principals of good nutrition and the importance of regular (but not excessive) exercise, the outcome was a fuller figure but improved mental and even physical health. She was also liberated from the torture of worrying about every calorie she consumed.

We all have to find sources of motivation and identify where our inspiration comes from. We also have to decide what kind of exercise we most enjoy or are willing to do and what foods we can live without—and abide by these decisions the majority of the time. Enjoying every minute of adherence isn't the objective. These behaviors for health are similar to taking out the garbage and flossing your teeth; neither may be a complete pleasure but they need to be done regardless and once they are, you appreciate the benefits and feel better for having done them. When our daughters watch us behave in ways that positively influence our health, they're more likely to do the same for themselves. Furthermore, they benefit from hearing us talk about these behaviors and practices in positive ways. Whether you're complaining about exercise and being aware of what you eat, or making your enthusiasm about your extra-long walk, kick-ass tennis game, or Lance Armstrong–like bike ride abundantly clear, your girl will register these moments in her data bank for future reference.

I am always on a diet. My mother took me to a dietician when I was in third grade because she thought I was fat and that she could help me lose weight. We never have anything but diet foods in our house because my mom is always on a diet too. She always talks about how fat she is, even though she goes to the gym everyday and eats nothing but diet stuff too.
— Stephanie, 13

Keeping an eye on your daughter's eating and exercise behaviors is part of conscientious parenting—and so is keeping an eye on your own. This doesn't mean developing an obtrusive vigilance that doesn't allow for her to make her own choices, which will sometimes include poor choices like fast food or candy for lunch. But it does mean making a point of noticing how she relates to food, how she approaches eating with others, and her general appearance. If any of the symptoms mentioned previously appear or if you have a concern about your daughter because something just doesn't feel right to you, you should discuss your observations and concerns with her.

Maintain a compassionate, nonjudgmental approach while holding on to your role and responsibilities as an involved parent. There's always the chance that she'll become defensive and dismiss your observations. But persevere if your intuition tells you to. Take her to a health care practitioner who can objectively assess her and either allay your fears or intervene on your behalf. And consider your own inner tapes. What are your comments about your own body and your thoughts about your daughter's physical appearance? Are you overly critical of how she looks, what she wears, and what she eats? Do you talk about the calorie content of food on a regular basis and are you restrictive about the foods you purchase, limiting your selections to diet, low-fat, and calorie-reduced choices? Is your diet constrained and repetitive and do you limit your intake to just a few categories of foods or very specific foods only? Spend some time seriously considering your own eating and exercise habits as well as your monologues and dialogues about your body and your feelings about how you look.

No discussion of teen body-speak would be complete without talking about fashion. The ever-changing modes of clothes that have marked each generation of teenagers throughout history have always reflected trends, ideas, and attitudes specific to young people in that time period. When it comes to teenagers, their choices in dress reflect four primary factors: their turmoil and fluctuating opinions about how they look, what part of themselves they feel deserves emphasis or not, their desire to carve out their own sense of self, and their expression of their sexuality. This all makes perfect sense in theory. In practice, however, the effects can provide powerful ammunition for the battles between mothers and daughters.

Girls' choices can trigger ferocious responses, including some of the most shaming and miserably immature rants an adult woman can unleash on her kid. What adults so easily forget is that "girls want to stand out by fitting in."[10]

Girls miss the real content of their mothers' responses because of the hurtful language and manner that often accompany the message. If a mother's true intention is to educate her daughter about the potential hazards of revealing her bosom or graphically accentuating her behind, or the off-putting aspects of black lipstick and nail polish, she absolutely must approach it with panache and humor. The big problem here is that, with rare exception, mothers just can't seem to find anything to be funny about. At these times, daughters are somehow a reflection of mothers themselves, and the battle becomes very personal.

At the risk of sounding like an uninformed fool, I must add that I am fully aware of the distress that some contemporary fashions can cause. I too have a daughter and I also specialize in the gynecological care of girls whose outfits can be downright peculiar but nonetheless in keeping with the fashions of their peers. I understand that mothers are responding to the dangers they perceive are present when a teen girl uses fashion to display body zones that mothers prefer to think of as fly-over states—breasts, buttocks, and the almighty pelvis. Low-cut blouses, tight pants, and hip-hugging waistbands that rest immediately above the pubic bone say: "I am *so* sexy" in a very loud voice. When mothers see their daughters eager and able to wear such things, they often respond in a critical voice that is as loud as their daughters' fashion statements.

True to experience and their desire to keep their girls safe, mothers know that such provocative choices can come with a high price. In a world that continues to objectify and sexualize women's bodies, adult women often know more than teenagers do about what can happen when inexperienced girls look and dress sexy.

The real mission here is figuring out how to convey the genuine risks of certain kinds of dress without humiliating your girls for feeling inclined to make those choices. Is looking sexy such a bad thing for girls? I'm not totally convinced it is, particularly given how sexy they often feel. But they need the counterpoint of the intelligence and life experience of their mothers, who can simply and calmly explain to them the factors involved when girls lead with their sexuality through their fashion choices.

Humor and creativity can go a long way in these complicated, difficult, and delicate situations. Further, talking about your point of view isn't the only way to convey a message. When you want to scream your head off and lock your daughter in her room for choosing what you perceive as "slut wear," consider exercising your creative forces to convey your point effectively while leaving a lasting impression.

I personally was beside myself with the provocative outfits my own daughter was wearing at 14. One day, in a new and different attempt at getting my point across, I imitated my daughter by wearing very tight jeans and a very low-cut blouse with cleavage visible from a mile away. When I then joined her to do yard work, my daughter was shocked and held nothing back in her expression of revulsion over my outfit. She said to me: "If you wear that, everyone is going to look at you." I responded by telling my daughter: "Gee, I say the same thing about you when you dress this way." After doing lawn work in this get-up for over an hour while Thalia was sweating at the prospect of my being spotted by her friends in our neighborhood, I relinquished my costume and changed into appropriate clothing for my age and size. My point was successfully conveyed, and my daughter began to change her clothing choices. The end result was we avoided a major altercation at the time and now, four years later, are able to laugh about this experience. This was, to be sure, one of my more creative and successful parenting moments.

A couple of years later, my daughter came to the breakfast table one school-day morning with an impressive amount of cleavage showing. I acknowledged how lovely she looked—if she were headed to an Elizabethan gala. She looked at me blindly so I came right out with it: "Thalia, the fruit, it's falling out of the fridge." I then took advantage of this teaching moment to mention that while her pleasure in her own appearance and sex appeal were entirely understandable—and evident by her choice of shirt—she could be so distracting to her teachers and classmates that they might not be able to accomplish their work. I suspect the sweatshirt she put on afterwards came off once she actually arrived at school. But the effort I made to avoid comments like "You look like a tramp" or "What do you think you're wearing, Missy?" resulted in a more instructive impression than hurling insults would have. My aim was to openly and calmly acknowledge her sexual energy without shaming her in the process and to give her an alternative perspective on how her choice of outfits might impact others.

Creative role playing or calm fashion commentary may not come to mind when your daughter is wearing something that strikes you as indecent and well beyond her age. Nonetheless, her desire to be perceived as sexually attractive and noticeable are the very forces involved in her decisions about what to wear. In and of itself, wanting to look one's sexual best is not a bad thing. In fact, it's predictable and appropriate for her stage of development. What is bad is for mothers to ignore this fact and then neglect mentoring their girls when it comes to reflecting on their fashion choices and the messages they convey.

If theatrical performances and measured responses don't come easily to you, there are other choices. Brief notes taped to mirrors or computer screens and general discussions about others like movie stars and singers, conducted in a noncombative, nonjudgmental tone, will be far more effective than emphatically preaching your opinions.

Any time a young woman deliberately accentuates her appearance with the primary intention of looking sexier, it is bound to be noticed by the world around her. After all, this is the point.

The book *Packaging Girlhood: Rescuing Daughter's from Marketer's Schemes* by Sharon Lamb and Lyn Brown sums it up this way:

> If she is dressing sexy for school to provoke remember that provocation is not always bad, and if we can help girls channel the desire to provoke, to draw attention to themselves, to make an identity statement in areas beyond fashion and sexuality, we will have opened up a myriad of possibilities for girl's development. The way to do this is not to prohibit, lay down the law, or tell them that their budding sexuality is unacceptable or makes them a target for violence. The way to do this is to understand why they are wearing what they're wearing and have meaningful conversations about the various influences that affect these

choices, as well as about the culture that sends them
a heavy dose of mixed messages about sexuality.[11]

Mothers are best off when they remember at all
times that their daughters' stage of development in no
way matches theirs. This is especially helpful when it
comes to fashions. Think about what she is trying to
accomplish and then compare it to where you are in
your own life. It will help reacquaint you with your role
and responsibilities.

If you are mothering a teenage girl, chances are high
that you are nearing or have actually entered your own
decade of turbulence and change, which is what I call
the ten years between the ages of 45 and 55. Changes are
inevitable for you, and if they occur during a daughter's
adolescence, it makes life all the more difficult.

According to national statistics compiled by the fed-
eral government, the average age of mothers at the time
their first baby is born has been steadily on the rise since
1970.[12] As a result of increased educational opportunities and increased opportunities in the workforce, more
women are delaying having children, with many waiting until their early 30s to begin raising a family. For
those of you who have had your first baby (or subsequent
pregnancies) between the ages of 30–38, your daughter's
adolescence will occur at the same time you're confronting middle age, or later.

The physical changes that mark middle age as well
as our reflections on sexuality and its place in our lives
in the past and present, can make our daughters' adolescence immeasurably arduous for both them and us. If
there was ever a time for a woman to have to take stock

of her own sexuality it's during her daughter's teen years. And if you're distressed about your sexuality at the same time, your distress can easily land right on top of your daughter's developing psyche.

Sometimes a mother's jealousy over her daughter's burgeoning and blatantly obvious sexual appetites, attractiveness, and access to sex is what drives a wedge between mother and teen. When this is the case, it is especially difficult for mothers to admit and manage. If you're a middle-aged woman who hates her middle-aged body and whose sex life is a thing of the past, it's awfully upsetting to be living with what can feel and seem like a teen sex kitten—especially if she resembles you at that time of your life.

Some mothers embrace a "well, if you can't beat 'em, join 'em" attitude, which can actually force their daughters to push against them with even greater force to succeed in their efforts to be distinct individuals. Ever wonder about moms who lose track of their age and adopt a look and feel similar to their teenager's? If you are inclined to search for look-alike fashions that remind you of something your daughter had on last week, it's time to seriously ask yourself: "What am I doing and why?"

Mothers who imitate the fashions trends in *Seventeen* magazine can create a war zone on the home front. These moms tip the balance of who is in charge of what and lose sight of their parental role, not to mention their age and decorum. The reasons this happens are varied—longings for the past, unhappiness in a sexless marriage, and uncontained envy are a few examples of reasons—not excuses—for this behavior. When a middle-aged woman streaks a strand of her hair pink, buys her accessories at

Aéropostale, and starts revealing deep cleavage, teen girls can feel justifiably mortified—and deeply anxious.

Girls want their mothers to look and act like responsible adults, a full generation ahead of them. They may not be able or willing to say this, but they are relying on us to maintain our role and responsibilities as their parents. This means giving them permission to swim freely as well as take chances in the deep end of the pool while keeping a watchful eye. Striking a balance between allowing this in combination with imposing rules and having them face consequences if they break them makes kids feel safer and more secure. This demands that we consider the extent of their expressions in clothing, style, and appearances with insight, maturity, good humor, and memories of what we used to wear to attract attention at their age. Before you decide what your absolute rules and regulations are, make sure you understand why you have them in the first place and what you intend to accomplish by enforcing them.

And remember that during this turbulent time, the best thing mothers can do for their daughters is to refer to the changes in their bodies as normal, reassure them about their maturation, continue setting excellent examples of a healthy lifestyle, and not overemphasize appearance—yours or theirs. Actively living a life that takes pleasure in sensual experiences including healthful behaviors enhances your daughter's understanding of and appreciation for her own body.

QUESTIONS TO ASK YOURSELF

There is no such thing as a perfect parent. But if you discover significant disparities between the choices you make in your own life and your expectation of your daughter's choices, this is the time to reflect on them and consider the impact this may have on her. A "don't do what I do, do what I say" message is ineffective and worth reconsidering for your sake and hers.

- How do I feel about my own body?

- Do I have healthy lifestyle habits that are visible to my daughter?

- Am I driven in an obsessive way to "eat right and exercise all the time"?

- Am I in competition with my daughter when it comes to fashion and clothes?

- Do I encourage my daughter to exercise frequently and regularly and do I abide by my own advice?

CHAPTER 3

THE SILENT WAR AGAINST AUTHORITY

"Parents are the bones on which children sharpen their teeth."

— Peter Ustinov

One of the hardest things to come to terms with as parents is that our children have their own minds and their own ideas. Adolescence is the time when teens test the limits and learn that their parents' authority is not absolute. They can make up their own minds, and frequently do, just for the pure thrill of it.

We begin to see evidence of this as they start to make choices about little things in early childhood. For example, when your three-year-old stomps her foot and insists on wearing her birthday hat to every meal, whether you're eating at home or not, it's kind of cute and everyone comments on her adorable willfulness and unique sense of style. However, as time passes and our girls start to put their foot down about things we think of as socially inappropriate behavior, the word *cute* is not what comes to mind.

As hard as it can be for parents, they must help their daughters win the war they wage against them; otherwise both kids and parents run the risk of serious consequences. Girls who face defeat against their parents can end up struggling with an undifferentiated self, lifelong confusion about who they independently perceive themselves to be, and what it is in life that would make them (not their parents) happiest. In other words, they risk experiencing a generalized failure to launch.

This can be disastrous when it comes to choosing a marriage partner, making a decision about having children, or selecting a profession. Women who weren't allowed and encouraged to individuate as teens and to make decisions based on who they are as separate individuals from their parents generally grow into women who can't articulate their own needs and wants, and live a life making choices to please everyone but themselves.

Adolescence is the time in your daughter's life when everything you say, do, or recommend will be scrutinized and field-tested in her effort to learn how to distinguish her likes and dislikes from yours. This is normal and, despite how difficult it may be for you to support, interfering with this process can put your daughter at risk for lifelong unhappiness and struggle.

Early on in your child's life, you and everyone else may have noticed your daughter's quick wit, great mind, and natural beauty. Perhaps she was one of those kindergarteners who taught herself to read and was funny and good at anything she tried. You started to make plans for the future. You had it all plotted out: terrific college opportunities from her stellar grades, competitive athletics, and volunteering for social justice causes in her spare time. A real Miss Perfect! You felt so proud of her so often—it was impossible to imagine this not being the case forever.

Then, something happens around her 12th birthday. She starts slinging mud at you for no apparent reason.

You feel alarmed and concerned. She'll turn on you at the drop of a hat and one stray glance in her direction might turn her into Medusa and you into stone. Her responses become completely unpredictable, and she seems to be using her talents and intelligence against you whenever she's given the opportunity.

Simultaneously, you might be frantically reading everything you can get your hands on to help you cope with her new and vexing behavior. The most striking feature of what you're reading is that it tells you that family remains critically important at this time. This makes no sense in the face of how your daughter is acting. It appears that your girl is increasingly disenchanted with her family and is challenging your family's traditions, rituals, beliefs, and authority. It's difficult to manage the volatile behaviors that degrade you and push you away. Furthermore, attack mode seems activated at all times, and you can feel how unsettled she is on a regular basis.

In addition, her unsettled behavior includes frequent tearfulness, bursts of anger, and exaggerated emotions reaching histrionic proportions that bear no resemblance to the easygoing child you've always known. You begin to wonder if someone switched places with your daughter when you weren't looking. You know, unequivocally, that *your* girl would never be acting this way!

As a midwife, I have been graced with the pleasure of handing many babies to their mothers for the first time. In all my years of doing so, I have yet to feel that babies and mothers are poorly or accidentally matched. We have the babies we are meant to have and they in turn have come to the families they are destined to be with, although the difficulties inherent in many of these relationships may lead us to believe otherwise. How we choose to manage these challenges, not the challenges themselves, is what makes for a productive and peaceful relationship between parent and child. This is especially true with mothers and daughters.

I have three daughters and in all three cases, 12 has been the year of absolute hell! Girls who are 12 are unpredictable, they lash out over the smallest thing and even do so in the middle of what you thought was a perfectly great conversation! They're very difficult to live with, and although I realize there is a hormonal factor at work, it's really hard to be patient and understanding when you feel beaten up over and over again.
— Gillian, 44

Teenage girls push hardest against what they are most familiar with and akin to—their mothers—and mothers often feel they take a beating for it. This is when the war against authority, authoritarianism, and authoritative behaviors starts to heat up.

Girls become resolute about lots of things around the age of 12. Listening to someone a generation behind you sermonize about virtually any topic that she has decided she is expert on can be both shocking and hilarious. Furthermore, these first signs of rebellion will almost always include content that is anathema to family politics, values, or customary practice. No matter how funny some of this actually is, the humor often gets lost in a mother's shock and dismay. Then annoyance and feelings of personal affront seem to seep in for many women as their daughter's rebelliousness accelerates.

Our society places great emphasis on individuality, independence, and self-reliance. We have self-help books, psychotherapists, and New Age practices that tout the importance of finding one's authentic and independent self. This emphasis on the inner self is encouraged from an early age, often eclipsing the identity of self that is more interdependent and part of a larger community of individuals or a member of a family.

When traits and characteristics of independence and self-reliance are exhibited by young children, parents and educators marvel at the maturity of the child and make a point of emphasizing such things in their descriptions of the child's healthy, if not precocious, character development. Independence has become a coveted merit badge and is highly regarded in our culture. It also becomes a measurement by which parents assess and compare their children to other people's kids. She who shows the most independence is the most exalted. No one wants a clingy kid or a crybaby!

Yet when our daughters' continued journey toward self-reliance and individuation begins to exclude us, relying less on our opinions and our approval, we mothers experience tremendous self-doubt, panic, and despair. In fact, our daughters' rebelliousness in their efforts to become their own person is one of the most difficult things mothers report as part of their parenting experience during their child's adolescence.

I have endured my own tedious, exhausting, and in the following case, life-threatening examples of rebelliousness in my teen daughter. The following story shows that no matter how clearly you state the rules, your daughter will probably break them. It's easy to become so overwhelmed with distress, rage, confusion, and fear that we would willingly take a leap from the nearest pier to end our suffering. In my case, I was thanking my daughter's angels for looking out for her while at the same time frantically searching for the best response to her behavior that would be instructive, rational, and appropriately disciplinary.

March 23, 2006, was the day my daughter got her driver's license. There's something very weird about being in the backseat of your car while your teenager is driving with a state trooper in the front next to her. Thalia was very nervous but did fine. *Shucks,* I thought, *here we go. I am going to be tied up in knots forever from this point forward.*

I had decided to give my 1993 240 Volvo station wagon to Thalia as her first car. It was paid off and seemed like the perfect choice for an inexperienced driver. The Swedes must have made these cars with teens in mind— they're as heavy as tanks and just as sturdy. If Thalia did have an accident she'd be well protected in that car. When I handed her the keys, I made it clear that she was only to drive around our county and not on the highway until she was more experienced. My car, my rules—or so I thought.

In New England, we often have strange episodic spring weather that hangs around for a few days in February and March, giving us all a much needed reprieve and reminder that even in the northeast, winter doesn't last forever. A spell like this occurred soon after Thalia got her license. The only difference this time was that this warm spell included an atypical rain so severe that there were flood warnings posted in our area. It was the kind of weather we all hate to drive in because of severely impaired visibility and the risk of hydroplaning.

It was a regular school day, but Thalia had requested a governor's pardon from attending. She told me she needed a mental health day, which I believe in now and again. With permission granted, I went off to work and she went back to bed. Later that afternoon, I got one of those feelings that I needed to talk to her—I couldn't explain why, but I just felt I should track her down and check in with her. I tried reaching her twice over a two hour period, but each time her cell phone went to voice mail. That was weird. I was sure she'd be catching up with Jerry Springer or something else that would keep her inside on a day like that. That was when I started to worry. We all know that sinking feeling where every possible disaster runs through your mind—fires, abduction, run-away situations, and, of course, auto accidents. How could I help it? She had just started driving.

Finally, two hours after my initial call I called back and Thalia answered. I knew immediately that something was . . . different. Her voice sounded a bit strange, and there was static in the background. She told me everything was fine, and although I suspected otherwise, whatever was happening was stuck in her throat. I decided to let sleeping dogs lie at that moment and just breathed a sigh of relief that she was alive and well enough to answer her phone. Maybe I'd get the information later, when I got home from work.

That night over dinner, we got on the subject of the weather. It was at this point that I discovered why my intuition had been up and running. Apparently Thalia had had a hankering to revisit the super-size lunch buffet table at a casino restaurant in Connecticut—two hours from home. Despite my clearly stated rules and the limits I had imposed on her driving, Thalia decided to use her mental health day to take a driving trip Unknowingly, I had granted my daughter all the permission in a torrential spring rain, to indulge herself and her best pal in the endless choices of savories and sweets offered at an all-you-can-eat buffet. In my usual calm style, I asked for confirmation of what I thought I had heard. And, as is my daughter's style, she matter-of-factly and shamelessly told me again where she had gone for lunch and went right on eating dinner.

Having been a midwife for so long and having been faced with life-threatening and stressful conditions, I have managed to cross-pollinate and apply my skills for staying calm under all sorts of other arduous conditions—this being one of them. I finally looked at my daughter and said, "Wow. So, how was the driving?" She looked up and said, "Pretty shitty. Yeah, actually it really sucked, especially on the highway." What was I supposed to do now?

I realized two things in that moment. First, a miss is as good as a mile, and I didn't need to have any details about the drive. Second, I needed to find a way to make it abundantly clear that this infraction wasn't tolerable and to convey this in such a way that my daughter would and could take my point without blocking the punch. This meant exercising great precision and brevity in my response. With an unswerving and giant hairy eyeball, I looked at my independent, fearless, and crazy teen girl and said, "How was lunch?"

There was so much more in this comment that an inquiry into her menu choices, and my daughter knew it. After I had listened to the description of scallops and dessert, I said in no uncertain terms, "Let me make myself perfectly clear. Don't ever do such a thing again, or I will take my car back, and you won't have wheels at all. End of discussion." That was all it took to convey my message unequivocally, and I knew it. If there's one thing teenage girls will turn off to immediately, it's their mother screaming her disapproval or spewing vitriolic fireballs at her for something she did that was dangerous and beyond stupid. If a mother does that, her daughter is more likely to repeat the performance and also miss the essence of the message because she turns you off from the get-go. Once you raise the level of cortisol, both of your brains are spinning and all channels of communication are closed for the foreseeable future.

When I was a little kid, my mother was always like, "Be independent, don't be afraid to be your own person, don't be a follower." But the second I started doing stuff she didn't approve of, she was like "Don't do it because I said so." But that isn't how she brought me up. It's very confusing.
— Alana, 16

The mixed messages we give teens about being independent are the result of a complicated combination of fear for their safety and a genuine longing for them to mature into independent and self-directed women. However, this creates tremendous tension in relationships between mothers and daughters and only escalates a teen's war against parental authority. I always wonder whether or not mothers notice the underlying message in their attempts to corral their kids. Don't parents realize that their efforts to maintain such tight controls over their daughters also speak loudly about a lack of confidence they have in their years of parenting before adolescence? By the time our kids have reached their early teens, much of the foundation for their development has been laid and they'll fall back on this for support as they individuate and grow up. A good portion of your foundational work is done by this time.

We often try to protect kids from making any mistakes. This should not be our objective. Instead, we need to help our daughters apply their independence and then cope with the consequences when, invariably, mistakes are made. This was my motive in telling my daughter that I would take her car away if she pulled another stunt like her out-of-town lunch excursion. It was a natural consequence for breaking an established rule. It wasn't necessary for me to scream and shout the consequence— just to state it and, most important, follow through with it if necessary. Attempting to protect our daughters from errors and the consequences of their decisions is futile and not in their best interests. Life is filled with mistakes and teens need to move through adolescence with an ever-growing ability to manage when the going gets rough. This is how they learn resilience, responsibility, and confidence in their own judgment.

The adolescent approach to gaining independence and selfhood can feel exaggerated and downright threatening to parents. The solution is not to actively resist but to establish fundamental, critically important, and impenetrable boundaries that your daughters cannot and will not advance beyond without their mothers' conscious approval. Set these boundaries carefully. These will be the bottom-line rules that you need to be prepared to defend no matter how aggressive, hysterical, or rebellious your daughter gets about keeping them. Once you've established these hard and fast rules, just sit back and watch where her efforts lead. But I warn you: be prepared to be put in situations over and over again that force you to restate the rules and stay as buoyant as possible in the face of challenges to the status quo. Just when you think they couldn't possibly do anything else as crazy as what they did last week, they will raise the bar on their own behavior and outdo themselves—yet again.

By the time my daughter was a senior in high school, I was well versed in her bravado, fearlessness, and ability to generate unique and provocative fun. After you've been in training for years with a girl like Thalia and you have your own natural ability to look at things with humor, it takes more than a minor infraction or off-color incident to leave you shocked or speechless. On the other hand, if your daughter does something so different from what you would ever do, it ups the ante for surprise. This is exactly what happened with Thalia's self-portrait for her senior art class. My daughter had the good judgment to reveal this to me post facto—a smart move under the circumstances.

One evening, she asked me to come into her room as she wanted to show me "a great photograph" that her best friend had taken. I went in with great anticipation and not a clue that I was about to face another sentinel moment in my experience as the parent of a delightfully feral teen girl. There it was on her computer screen: a photograph of my daughter, completely in the buff, sitting in a chair at our local bookstore, posed with a coffee table book on her lap positioned in such a way so as to conceal her breasts and "Miss Kitty." She looked awfully studious on first pass. But, once I put it all together—my daughter, naked, in our small-town bookstore, posing for a photograph—I actually was speechless.

Once I composed myself, I calmly asked my daughter to please explain what was going on . . . and why! She was happy to oblige and proceeded to describe how she and her pal were oh, so careful to make sure the coast was clear before she whipped off her full-length parka and sat down with her book for the big moment. Then came the news that she had submitted this to her art teacher (a terrific and insightful fan of my daughter's) as her self-portrait. As it turned out, she received an A on this assignment. She told me her teacher said, "You know, this is terrific! A self-portrait is supposed to express and reveal all sides of a person, and this shows so much about who you really are!" To be sure.

So there I was with no idea what to do with all this information. I was happy about her A in art class; stunned by her combination of creative energy, imagination, and chutzpah; and relieved that she hadn't been caught in the act. I decided to focus on the positives—that I was not only impressed with her final grade but also very happy that she had pulled off this caper without a hitch. I also threw in that I would have been upset if I had been notified by the police that she had been stealing from the bookstore rather than sitting in it naked. I decided to leave it at that. I quickly realized that this incident, albeit dramatic and daring, was essentially harmless and could be filed under "wild for wild's sake." No one was killed, harmed, or arrested, and my daughter didn't steal!

While driving through a monsoon to a casino buffet or stripping down in the local bookstore are obvious ways for your teenage daughter to rebel, there are also much more subtle decisions that she will make at this time in her life. Unexpected announcements about adopting health and lifestyle practices in direct opposition to yours are your daughter's way of expressing her individuality and learning more about her desires in general. These announcements aren't necessarily timely. In fact, poor delivery of information is a specialty of teens. They exhibit extraordinarily poor timing when it comes to letting you know things that may be important. It's a reflexive fear response combined with immaturity—not evidence of a plot designed to make you lose your mind.

Telling you that she has become a vegetarian as you're pulling a beautiful roast out of the oven for Sunday dinner or announcing that she's joined the track team after you've just spent three days organizing your schedule in order to get her to the dance classes she begged you for are perfect examples. You have the choice to respond to these things in two ways: you can either blow your top, which is likely to result in some sort of altercation, or you can take a deep breath and remind yourself that her declining your roast is not about you but about her needing to be different from you. Simply offer her more vegetables and remind her that there's always peanut butter and jelly to supplement her dinner.

In addition, it's a good idea to ask her why she's made such a choice and to pay attention to what she says. You may very well discover her new best friend or love interest is a vegetarian. Or you may be let in on other secrets, like how her newfound dietary habits are allowing her passage into a deeper understanding of her body that you never would have imagined were linked to her new rejection of the once-loved hamburger.

I told my mom I didn't want to eat dairy products anymore. She got all upset and started preaching at me about calcium and quick, easy protein. What she didn't understand was dairy makes me feel sick. Finally, we had a conversation about it and we both realized that I was lactose intolerant, and we made some decisions together about ways to get enough protein without dairy.

— Tracy, 16

What your daughter believes is good for her physical health and well-being may be the polar opposite of what you have in mind. The point is not whether it pleases you but whether or not it is helping her become a separate person and isn't harmful to her, or, as in Tracy's case, is actually in her best interest.

Invariably, the world will be filled with lightning rods for your daughter's kooky teenage behavior. Eating a vegan diet, dressing in goth fashions, pursuing a career as a model for Maybelline, or following a boyfriend around the world—all have equal standing as options for your daughter if they represent the opposite of anything you happen to be or do. These new interests and devotional practices can throw mothers off balance in a New York minute and leave them feeling deeply unsettled. Daughters sense the build-up of their mother's anxiety and come back at them with tremendous fury in an effort to secure their own position.

Rather than arguing with your daughter in an effort to win every battle, the better response is to listen attentively and avoid escalating the situation by arguing with her about what she doesn't know. I realize that she may be assuming a degree of authority that she can't possibly have after only 12 or so years of life, more than half of which has been spent functionally illiterate. However, if you respond by flexing your authoritarian, "I am your mother" muscle, you're sure to end up in a brawl that will serve no purpose and will worsen the strife. Instead, act like a real authority. Assess all content, discern what really requires a response, devise an appropriate rebuttal, and move from a place of sturdiness and confidence— which being an expert and authority should have granted you after all this time.

QUESTIONS TO ASK YOURSELF

The following questions are designed to help you reflect on the rules imposed on you as a teen girl and compare them to the rules you have now created for your own daughter. Review them with the retrospective knowledge you have from your own experiences in adolescence, and let that experience guide you regarding how you're parenting in the present. Ask yourself if you're simply repeating your mother's style or have you designed limitations and rules based on what's appropriate and applicable to your own daughter and the times we're living in.

- How did you feel about the way your mother exercised her rules and regulations?

- How did you feel about the rules themselves?

- In retrospect, which of your mother's rules made sense and which didn't? Why and why not?

- What rules do you consider the most important ones for your daughter to abide by and why?

- What consequences does your daughter experience when she breaks your rules? Are these consequences working?

- Do you have enough rules or too many?

CHAPTER 4

JUST THE FACTS, MA'AM

"From the moment I was six I felt sexy. And let me tell you it was hell, sheer hell, waiting to do something about it."

— Bette Davis

Most mothers consider having sex to be one of the boundaries that their teen daughters must not cross, under any circumstances. Many mothers, much like their teenage daughters, consider themselves to be authorities on the subject of sex, but this may not be the case at all. If you're a mother who keeps shoving your opinions about sex down your daughter's throat, this may very well work against her healthy development—including her continued development of independence and self-reliance. If you feel that sex for your teen daughter is absolutely off-limits, then the war against your presumed authority will definitely show up here.

This morning at breakfast, Mom got on some big discussion of sex and was talking about a friend of hers who was teaching a sex orientation course. She threw in how it was someone's privilege and not a right and how bad it was that so many young women were sexually involved at such a young age. Needless to say, she was directing it right to me. So, I got up and washed the dishes instead of listening.

— Yolanda, 15

Regardless of a mother's values about sex, she has a responsibility and an obligation to acknowledge that sexual identity formation, sexual activity, and intimate partnership are important components of teen development, and the first steps toward becoming a sexually healthy adult. The likelihood that a teen girl will grow into a sexually healthy and satisfied woman increases dramatically when her mom is willing to face the fact that her teenage daughter is thinking about sex and able to give her the information and help she needs to explore this part of herself safely and without shame.

Establishing yourself as well informed and truly fluent on the subject of teens and sex during your daughter's early adolescence is a very good idea. Providing a loving and accurate authority for your daughter to rely upon during these first tentative stabs at revolution and independence gives your daughter the message that you love her whether she is sexually active or not, and that you are there for her if she gets in over her head. Isn't this what we all want our teen girls to understand?

Before you can assume the role of a well-informed and loving authority for your daughter, you must be truly knowledgeable and devoted to the dissemination of real, factual information—not terrified imaginings or chosen moral values. Misinformation and myths about sex and risks associated with teen sex abound and are especially rampant in the minds of fearful parents. Despite the enormous amount of accurate information available through books, the Internet, and films, parents a generation behind their kids are often the ones with the least information about human sexuality. And yet they're the first to preach that their girls should remain virginal.

With rare exception, the monologues parents have on the value and imperative of maintaining virginity are based on values about sex and chastity, not in sound public health information. Sex and morality are an uneasy mix and can create mayhem in even the calmest, most functional families. Many of my patients' mothers were deeply stunned and disappointed when they learned that their daughters were sexually active. The responses can range from tears and panic to raging fury in the blink of an eye.

I didn't really expect it to happen. I knew he liked me and I liked him but we weren't planning on having sex. Then we were together at this party and it just happened. We didn't use a condom and I didn't have anything for birth control. It was my first time. I freaked out that I could be pregnant and knew that I couldn't say anything to my mom. She would have been so mad! A girl at school has a mother who is a nurse and really cool about sex. She told me I could call her so I did and she told me to get the "morning-after pill" from Planned Parenthood. She helped me figure out what my chances of being pregnant were. She was pretty easy to talk to. I could never talk to my mother about this. She's made it clear, in all sorts of ways, that she thinks having sex is bad and that if I did have it I would really be disappointing her.
— Emma, 14

I was shocked and devastated when I found out that my daughter had lost her virginity at the age of 17. She was at a party with other students from the boarding school she attends and the boy was someone she knows from school. It felt so risky to me. What happens if she has contracted a sexually transmitted infection? And I couldn't even bring myself to ask her if she used protection for pregnancy. I can barely talk about it.

— Debbie, 42

In these situations, I do my best as a health care provider (and sympathetic mother of a teen) to set the stage for the separation of values from facts. I know, as a midwife who is generally better informed than the mother I am talking to, that dividing the two issues is helpful to a mother whose head is spinning with terror that her girl has "run into trouble" simply because she's had sex. I also try to help moms understand that daughters need to be allowed to make some of their own decisions, even if they are less than perfect. We can offer them counsel and guidance, but we must let them remain independent with the adult understanding that this means we won't be making their decisions for them. This is what genuine authorities do. It is also what good mentors do when they're working with folks less experienced than they are.

This is, of course, easier for parents to say than do. It places them in the tenuous situation of letting their teenager make independent decisions for which they as their parents may ultimately be held responsible. This can be particularly problematic when it comes to bad decisions about sex. This is why the division of facts from values is especially important as sexual activity commences or is near commencing. It is facts, not values, that ultimately help girls avoid or manage unintended or undesirable outcomes.

In order to better understand the actual difference between values about sexual activity and facts about sex, review the list below. As you read, you'll see how similar values and misconceptions can become and how removed they can then be from facts. Try creating a list of your own to help you clarify your own opinions and knowledge about sex and see how it compares to the one in this chapter.

Value: Sex should only be experienced with someone you really love.

Fact: Really loving someone does not necessarily determine someone's experience of enjoyment and pleasure.

Value: Having sex with multiple partners puts you at risk for remaining single as an adult because no one will want to partner with you.

Fact: Multiple partners at this time in history, especially in the absence of safe-sex practices, places you at a higher risk for sexual transmitted infections, but does not increase your chances of remaining single or unpartnered as an adult.

Value: Having sex with multiple sexual partners has no purpose and only puts women at risk for contracting an STI.

Fact: Many women report that they are happy to have had more than their marriage partner as a sexual partner and that having had the experience of varying sexual styles helped them establish a stronger sense of their sexual identity and criteria for sexual satisfaction.

Value: Oral and anal sex practices are only done by aberrant individuals and are not included in normal human sexual behaviors.

Fact: Both men and women enjoy oral and anal sexual activity and, based on my experience talking to men and women of all sexual persuasions, they fall within the realm of normal human sexual expression.

Value: None of the birth control methods on the market today are really very safe or effective so sex should be avoided for that reason alone.

Fact: The only birth control methods that are 100 percent effective and safe are abstinence, a same-sex partner, or masturbation. However, many contraceptive methods available today are very safe and effective and provide excellent pregnancy prevention. Further, using more than one method simultaneously (e.g., condoms and oral contraceptives) is nearly 100 percent effective and involves both heterosexual partners in taking responsibility for their behavior.

Value: The love relationships that teens have are never deep enough or meaningful enough for them to include sex. And anyway, all teen boys really want is to have sex with girls and then dump them.

Fact: The love affairs that girls and boys have in high school are often very meaningful to them. In fact, many people in long-term loving marriages met and fell in love when they were in high school. And it is absolutely not true that all that teen boys want is to have sex with girls. Many teen boys fall deeply in love with their girlfriends (or boyfriends), just as their girlfriends fall very much in love with them.

The responsibility for knowing essential and basic information about teen sex, including where to get appropriate health care in your area, falls on mothers. In addition, mothers need to be willing to talk with teens using teen language, in part so both parties will actually understand what is being communicated.

It took me a while as a midwife to learn the language and develop the skills to communicate comfortably and effectively with sexually active teens. It was difficult in the beginning to figure out how best to approach them when it came to specific questions about their health that were related to their sexual activity. When it comes to drug use and sex, teens are, naturally, evasive and teen girls who are having sex are worried about the judgment they'll encounter from you. Once you build up trust and form a partnership with them, it's easier for them to tell you things you need to know. They need to feel unequivocally that you're their advocate before they'll tell you the complete truth. This story from early on in my practice is a perfect example of this. I learned so much from this patient and have been able to use that experience throughout my years in practice and as a mother to my own teenager.

Iris was 16 when we first met in her fourth month of pregnancy. She was a tough inner-city kid who came to her appointment with her boyfriend. She would barely give me the time of day and instead sat on her beau's lap during our visit, preoccupying herself with fixing his braids. She was at an important stage of her pregnancy and I needed her undivided attention, but she wasn't particularly interested in giving it. She finally came to when she remembered a question she had about something in her mouth—bumps she had never seen before and was wondering about.

To me, the bumps on her tongue looked like they might be condyloma—venereal warts caused by the human papillomavirus, more commonly known as HPV. Although not common in non-HIV infected patients, these warts can occur in people who regularly have oral sex with an HPV-positive partner without using a condom.

I needed to find out if there was a possibility that I was looking at something more complicated than large taste buds, which was my other thought. I delicately asked Iris: "So do you two enjoy fellatio on any regular and frequent basis?" This got me absolutely nowhere. She responded to my question with a look of confusion and arrogant dismissal. She had no idea of what I was talking about. Finally, after several attempts at rewording my question and out of sheer and desperate frustration I resorted to a more direct line of questioning: "Iris, do you ever put your boyfriend's cock in your mouth?" What a showstopper that was. The two of them were stunned.

The hair salon activity came to a screeching halt and then they both answered my question thoroughly, allowing me greater ability to diagnose the problem. Luckily for Iris, the sour candy that was an unfortunate staple of her diet was the cause of her bumps—a.k.a. enlarged taste buds, not HPV-related warts.

Although the initial impact of my direct and explicit line of questioning was off-putting, the relationship I was able to develop with Iris—because of my willingness to ask my question directly combined with my apparent comfort with the possible answer—provided a foundation for direct communication between us from that point forward. After that, Iris requested me for most of her prenatal visits and, as it turned out, I was on call when she went into labor. Our experience as laboring woman and midwife was powerful and cemented our fondness for each other.

Years later, this young woman has a special place in my heart. I learned an important lesson about caring for adolescents: you must talk with them directly, without a tone of judgment in your voice, and in a language they can make sense out of. You have to do this from the very beginning of your conversations with them. Although Iris was my patient, the same has held true for me as a mother. Mothers should keep this in mind when they're talking to their daughters about sex. Believe it or not, it makes you more credible.

Once mothers are on solid ground regarding their communication skills, factual knowledge about the real risks of sexual activity, and have access to information about sexual health and safety, then and only then should their values about teen sex be declared. It's only once the facts are fully understood by mothers that their values can be the least bit helpful—which is, after all, the point in conveying your values in the first place.

Even if you are the mom of a girl who has told you that she genuinely chooses to delay having sex regardless of what her friends are doing, you still need to provide information about sex, because teenagers are unpredictable and can change their minds on a dime.

I had been seeing Janet for management of her painful periods for a couple of years. She was 16 when she first came to me and she made it clear to me that she really wasn't planning on becoming sexually active until much later in her teens. She told me that she took sex very seriously and wasn't like many of her friends who she felt treated sex lightly.

She wasn't crazy about the idea of taking birth control pills to manage her severe cramps and heavy bleeding, and because of her feelings about being sexually active, she didn't need the contraceptive benefit. So we came up with alternatives that she could use during months when her periods were especially troublesome. We agreed she'd keep track of her periods so she could stay one step ahead of her severe cramps by using anti-inflammatory medications before the onset of her menses. I also referred her for acupuncture and instructed her in acupressure massage techniques that she could use on herself for pain management.

One day, I noticed she had made an appointment to see me. I hadn't seen her for several months, so I assumed that her symptoms had worsened or that our plan wasn't working. When we started to talk, she explained that although she hadn't planned on having sex, her feelings had changed when she met her current boyfriend. As she put it: "At first, I wasn't so sure that we loved each other. But, even though that wasn't so clear, I really wanted to have sex with him. And so I did. It's not what I expected would happen but it did."

The remainder of our visit was spent talking about how normal her feelings were and that perhaps using birth control pills and condoms would be a good idea now, given how her feelings had changed. She agreed and left with a prescription and a follow-up appointment in three months.

This story is a perfect example of how a girl's feelings can change, and then she's faced with a situation she didn't expect. Not long before this happened, Janet was full of conviction that was pointing her in an opposite direction from where she was only a few months later.

Changing their minds isn't the only reason girls end up having sex with someone when they weren't planning on it. Regularly in my midwifery office I find myself managing the unexpected outcome of coerced sexual experiences happening to unsuspecting and uninformed girls. They usually have absolutely no preparation for the possibility of such a thing as rape and how best to avoid it. This is an aspect of sexuality that no one talks about in earnest in an attempt to help their daughters avoid such experiences. As a midwife, I see these teens post facto when they and their mothers are at their worst. Both mothers and teens are scared and worried and feel completely blindsided by the event.

Tina was a 15-year-old whose older sister brought her to me after she had been raped by the brother of a friend. Tina had been spending the night at her friend's house after a big party and this was when the incident occurred. Neither Tina nor her sister really knew what to do, but because Tina's sister was my patient, she brought her to see me. They were terrified and, to make matters worse, Tina had developed symptoms of a STI and was beside herself with fear that she had contracted something life-threatening. She was already on birth control pills for acne treatment so the fear of pregnancy was (fortunately) not in the mix. I did a pregnancy test anyway, for the sake of further reassurance, and I tested for STIs. It turned out that Tina had contracted trichomonas, an infection that is curable with a specific antibiotic.

Once my exam was over, it was time for me to discuss strategies for emotional management of what had happened and to give Tina and her sister information to reduce the risks of either of them ever experiencing something like this again. This involved sympathetic straight talk. I gave them the facts about sexual assault in the United States—our rates of sexually violent crimes against women exceed those of many of the developed nations of the world, including Germany, Japan, and England. In addition, over 70 percent of assailants are known to their victims. Girls and women are most often sexually assaulted by friends, family members, teachers, coaches, and people they work with. In addition, not all victims report these crimes so our estimates are presumably lower than the actual number of crimes that occur each year.[1] Sharing this information was a critical part of my care plan, intended to reduce Tina's shame and humiliation over what had happened. Often, a woman blames herself for the assault and feels that this kind of thing is rare and not experienced by many other women.

Sadly, as the statistics above demonstrate, this is not at all the case. We then talked about creating a safety plan that involved Tina calling her sister to pick her up any time she felt at risk as well as other forms of prevention.

At the end of her appointment, I gave Tina a prescription for medication for her infection and empowering information to keep herself safer from sexual violence in the future. Both she and her sister were relieved, and they left my office with less fear and more confidence about their ability to avert this situation again.

This is an example of the kind of sex education that girls must have. The best person to get it from is their mother.

Parents of teenage girls often jump to the conclusion that if their teen girls become sexually active they will inevitably contract a sexually transmitted infection. This concern isn't totally unfounded, as the rates of some STIs are highest among teen girls. A recent study of teen girls between the ages of 14–19 noted that one out of every four teenagers in this age group has had at least one sexually transmitted infection.[2] Tina was a case in point, but she was also the victim of sexual assault, which parents almost never discuss with their girls. The fact is, most parents don't really know the facts about STIs or have current information about real risks. They don't know which teens are most likely to be infected and why, what infections teens are at greatest risk for, how these infections are actually transmitted, and how high the risks are for their particular kid. Pressing the "STI alarm" or shouting from a rooftop about the inevitability of contracting a STI when talking to girls about sex will get you absolutely nowhere when it comes to prevention.

So here are the facts about STIs and teens. Note: this information is not intended to scare you but to help you feel more informed and as a result more realistic about what could happen, instead of worrying that a life-threatening infection awaits your daughter every time she walks out of the door.

HUMAN PAPILLOMAVIRUS (HPV)

Despite the fact that HPV has been around for years and is known to have potentially life-threatening consequences if undetected and left untreated, it wasn't until a vaccine was developed to prevent the infection and recommended for girls in middle school that any dialogue about the most common STI began between parents, health care professionals, and teens.

HPV is the most prevalent STI affecting teenage girls. In one recent study of three million teen girls, HPV was found in 18 percent of participants, showing no higher prevalence among one socioeconomic or ethnic group over another.[3] While many parents have their hair on fire about the risks of their daughters contracting HIV/AIDS, it's HPV they should concern themselves with most of all, and yet many don't even know it exists.

There are multiple strains of the virus with effects that vary in severity from annoying and unsightly venereal warts (which are essentially benign) to those that can cause cervical cancer. Women between the ages of 20–24 are at highest risk for infection, although girls 14–19 come in a close second.[4] Whatever the age, HPV can have far ranging effects for women and estimates from the Centers for Disease Control are that 80 percent of all women will be infected by multiple strains of the virus by age 50.[5]

In most cases, the course is like that of other viruses, including the flu: people become infected, the virus runs its course, and no permanent damage occurs. And, like the flu, because HPV is viral, there is no antibiotic to cure it. However, unlike the flu, HPV can remain dormant in the body and resurface after long periods of time, potentially resulting in abnormalities that occur long after someone's original exposure has taken place.

Detection of HPV infection occurs in two ways. First, if someone develops venereal warts, it is apparent that they've been exposed, at least, to the strain(s) of HPV that cause(s) warts. Although the warts themselves are harmless, their presence indicates the high probability of having been exposed to additional strains of the virus, including those that can cause cervical cancer. Doing a Pap smear on teens and women who have been and/or are currently sexually active will help to determine exposure to HPV and can provide information regarding the need for further evaluation, including additional testing or treatment.

Abstaining from sex with male or female partner(s) with HPV would be an ideal and effective method of prevention. However, this is far easier said than done. Detection in men and women can be difficult and is certainly not on the minds of lustful teens who may be unaware or under-aware of the risks. In women, venereal warts are often visible to the naked eye and/or easily felt by the woman herself. There are many smooth skin surfaces of the vulva and vaginal opening that make it relatively easy to detect their presence, even if they're small. However, on the wrinkled shaft of a flaccid or even erect penis these tiny warts are often invisible to both the infected individual and untrained examiner. Additionally, there are so many men and women who are infected that the virus is now considered endemic in our population and not even monogamy is necessarily protective if your first sexual partner in life has had two or more previous partners.[6] Condoms, familiarity with your partner's sexual history, and an understanding of how the virus is spread are your best defenses against HPV infection.

Generally, teenage girls (and adult women) are relatively unaware of HPV and its potentially serious side effects, despite the fact that it is so common. It's often not until a teen has an abnormal Pap smear that she learns anything about the virus. This is also how mothers often find out for the first time that their daughters are sexually active.

Each week, I review results of laboratory tests that I have ordered on patients the week before. Essentially, I am looking for abnormal findings that I have to inform patients about and recommend treatment for. Because of the prevalence of HPV, it's not uncommon to have an abnormal Pap smear in my pile of papers. If the Pap smear was done on a teen patient, I probably will be talking with the girl's mother after I speak with her. No matter how much conflict girls have with their moms, they will often go to their mothers immediately if they feel something is seriously wrong with them—especially when it involves their physical health.

Kathy was 15 and I had seen her for a gynecological exam and prescribed birth control pills for contraception. She told me she had been sexually active with more than one male partner and didn't always use condoms. I performed a Pap smear and other STI screening tests. Her Pap smear came out mildly abnormal, so I contacted her to have her repeat her Pap smear in four months to make sure her abnormalities weren't worsening. As is often the case with teen girls, Kathy responded dramatically to my call, and convinced she had some lethal form of something or other, burst into tears on the phone, and was positively inconsolable. I suggested she come back in to talk with me in person. She asked if she could bring her mother with her. I assured her that this was entirely up to her. I knew what was coming; it was going to be one of those visits where I have to mediate between an unsuspecting mother and a scared out of her wits teen who is fairly certain the end of her life is near—if not because of the STI she might have then because her mother will kill her when she finds out she's been having sex.

Kathy and her mother came into my office and things were very tense between them. Her mother was downright belligerent; as for Kathy, she had shrunk about three inches from her statuesque five foot eight height and looked strangely dwarfed against her madder-than-hell mom. I explained my findings to both Kathy and her mother in the simplest terms I could, but the reality that HPV is an STI was impossible to conceal. After all, how else would this virus have infected Kathy's cervix?

When the cat was out of the bag and the fact of her daughter's sexual activity was unequivocal, her mother simply fell silent and turned her head, like a poisonous snake might when retreating into a hole or making preparations to bite and kill. In this case, it was a bit of both. It was the first phase of the silent treatment, and the look of dread on Kathy's face made me want to cry. I knew this kid was really in for it when she left my office. This is a common scene in my work with teens: it comes from feeling completely shocked by something that's actually rather common—a sexually active teen in the age of HPV.

Despite the ad campaign for the vaccine designed to prevent infection, the adoption of the slogan "I Want to be One Less" as a promotional tool has done less than it ideally could to inform the masses of the existence and risks associated with HPV. More often than not, teens and their mothers ask me to translate what "one less" means, as it is so vague.

When a Pap smear is more than mildly abnormal, a diagnostic procedure called a colposcopy may be necessary if the abnormality may have been caused by one or more strains of HPV that can cause cervical cancer. A colposcopic exam is a regular medical office procedure that utilizes an instrument called a colposcope. The colposcope magnifies the surface of the cervix, allowing the examiner to visualize the tissues closely to determine if they appear abnormal on a cellular level. Should suspicious areas be seen, small samples (biopsies) of tissue are collected. The procedure takes approximately 15–30 minutes and is performed in a clinic or medical office by someone trained in colposcopic exam techniques. Depending on the pathological findings of the biopsies, treatments will be recommended and can range from simply repeating the Pap smear in four months to cervical surgery. Surveillance and follow-up through repeated Pap smears at recommended intervals are always part of the follow-up plan, and patients are wise to follow their practitioners' advice.

Results of a recent large study revealed that regular condom use did dramatically reduce the risks of both contracting and spreading the HPV virus.[7] Although HPV can be spread by skin-to-skin genital contact, it is penile-vaginal intercourse or anal intercourse without a condom that present the highest risk for contracting the virus.

CHLAMYDIA

Chlamydia is the second most common STI among teen girls, affecting 5 percent of all girls ages15–24.[8] Surveillance data from the Centers for Disease Control for 2006 showed an increase in reported cases over 2005 and the majority of those infected were teen girls. Actual cases are estimated to be even higher as many girls are not routinely screened for the infection, even when they present for gynecological care.[9]

For teen girls, infection with chlamydia presents serious problems and many undiagnosed cases remain in the reproductive tract for long periods of time. Undiagnosed chlamydia infections can lead to pelvic inflammatory disease (PID), infertility problems, and possibly sterility. At present, I don't work in a community with a high prevalence of chlamydia, but I still do routine screening on every woman I see who is 25 and under, regardless of her relationship status. The following experience occurred after I had been practicing for over 15 years in the same community and confirmed my belief in routine screening.

A friend and co-worker in her mid-20s came to see me for her annual gynecological exam. I knew many details of her private life, including that she had been in a monogamous heterosexual relationship for more than one year. She and her partner were content, although she wasn't convinced this was her true love. He was also headed toward a new job in another state. They decided to see how this change would affect their feelings for each other and go from there.

My friend had denied any health concerns or symptoms and I proceeded with my normal exam. This included a cervical culture for chlamydia. A week later, I was reviewing my paperwork from the lab and discovered that her test was positive. Neither of us had had any reason to suspect she might be infected. Like many women, she had no symptoms of the infection and neither did her partner. There was also no real way of knowing how long she had been infected or whom she contracted the infection from. I treated both her and her partner and then had her return for a repeat culture to make sure that the medication had worked.

Chlamydia can be contracted in the cervix, mouth, or anus but it is most common in the cervix as a result of heterosexual intercourse. Unlike HPV, it is bacterial and can therefore be treated and cured with an antibiotic. Repeating the test for detection to determine if the treatment was effective is always recommended. In addition, many practitioners, myself included, will treat partners, if accessible or present, in an effort to prevent spread or re-infection with the bacteria. Teens are often "serially monogamous." In other words, while they may only have one partner at a time, their length of stay with that partner is likely to be relatively short. Therefore, in an effort to reduce rates of infection, it's not a bad idea to extend treatment to a patient's sex partner (male or female) if the partner has accompanied the patient to the appointment. According to state public health laws, chlamydia is a reportable disease: every positive diagnosis that's made in laboratory testing must be reported to the state health department, which allows for highly accurate accounting of rates of infection. This is assuming practitioners test patients in the first place, which is not always the case.[10] Nationwide, chlamydia infections are rising in teen girls. As a consequence, routine testing is recommended for all women 25 and under when they present for gynecological care.

Diagnosing chlamydia has gotten easier and is now possible through a first-morning urine test. Peeing into a cup—it's that simple and highly accurate. Treatment is a single dose of an oral antibiotic and is highly effective. Condoms (once again) when worn for intercourse, anal sex, or oral sex provide a barrier that makes it nearly impossible for the bacteria to be transmitted.

Herpes Simplex Virus (HSV)

Whenever people hear the word herpes, the look of alarm on their faces is enough to consider calling 911. This is a direct reflection of their lack of knowledge about herpes and how common it is in people of all ages. Herpes viruses are common to kids, teens, and adults. Some are transmitted through sexual contact and some are not. There are eight herpes viruses known to be infectious to humans. Anyone who has ever contracted chicken pox or shingles has had one of the eight. The herpes infections we'll be talking about here are called HSV I and HSV II.

Determining if someone has strain I or II can only be accomplished by doing a culture of a sore that is present. Both strains can infect the mouth and/or the genitals as a result of intimate and/or sexual activity. Those of you who have had a cold sore on your mouth or lip may not know it, but that cold sore is probably the result of HSV I. Although we often just call these oral sores "cold sores," they are in fact herpes infections, and many people afflicted with these troublesome, painful, and unsightly sores aren't aware of the causative infectious agent.

You can infect someone else with herpes if you have a cold sore that's clearly visible, one that is almost gone or even (much less likely) when no cold sore is present at all. If you're a person with herpes and you kiss someone on the mouth or on the genitals when you have an existing sore or one that's almost healed, it's probable that you'll spread the virus to the person you kissed and to the part of their body you were kissing. Genital infections with HSV I run a course that often, but not always, begins with a primary outbreak that can be very uncomfortable and in some cases downright hellish. A painful sore (or sores) on the genitals accompanied by fever and flulike symptoms (including body aches and fatigue) are common with an initial outbreak and can last for several days. This can be terrifying for the unsuspecting and uninformed teen (or adult) who had no idea that their partner had HSV I or even what it is, for that matter.

Teenagers whose sexual activity has been kept secret face a real challenge if they find themselves in this position. If a girl becomes systemically ill and finds a sore on her genitals that erupts within seven to ten days after having had sex, seeking help from a parent who is unaware of her sexual activity only compounds her terror and the severity of her symptoms. If an unsuspecting and uneducated girl becomes really sick from a primary herpes infection, she can easily jump to the conclusion that she's dying. Should the symptoms of her initial infection become severe, it becomes a matter of "pick your poison": tell your parent about your sexual activity and that now you think you're dying from it, or prepare for an early and miserable death all alone! In the mind of a teenage girl, the natural flare for drama, fear of discovery about her sexual activity, and lack of awareness of what is likely happening to her body—in combination with the sheer physical misery of her symptoms—can make for a *very* difficult time.

Asking a partner whether or not they have herpes before you have sex with them is a great prevention strategy. However, it rarely happens with sexually active people of any age. Furthermore, not many people, including those who know they have cold sores, understand what the infection is, how it is spread, or when they are contagious.

Treatment for an initial outbreak includes comfort measures for the pain of the genital sores as well as oral antiviral medication. These medications shorten the course of the outbreak but can't kill the virus. As is the case for all viruses, there is no antibiotic treatment available that eradicates the infection. Antiviral medication for herpes reduces the severity and length of the outbreak by suppressing the virus's multiplication, encouraging it to become dormant more quickly. Nonetheless, it is always possible for the virus to rear its head again at some point in the future. In the case of HSV I, future outbreaks on the genitals or transmission are less likely than if someone has been infected with HSV II in the genital area.[11]

Although overall rates of herpes infections are decreasing, rates of genital infection attributable to HSV I are increasing. This may be related to the rise in oral sex among teens and a general lack of awareness of how the infection is spread through oral-genital contact.

HSV II, commonly thought of as genital herpes, can and usually does infect the genitalia but can also infect other regions of the body, including the mouth. When herpes II is spread through genital-to-genital contact, especially heterosexual intercourse, girls are more likely to contract the infection than boys. A primary outbreak of genital herpes from HSV II is generally not as severe as one from HSV I. The same symptoms will appear but to a lesser extent and most people are simply not as sick from a primary outbreak if the viral strain is HSV II. This is good news. The bad news is that repetitive outbreaks are more common when HSV II is the infecting agent.[12]

The primary intervention for reducing the likelihood of infection is understanding how the infection is transmitted between partners during oral, genital, and/or anal contact. Using condoms and limiting the number of sex partners can reduce the risks.

In my opinion, it's not unreasonable to start educating kids early on about the value of not sharing drinking glasses, silverware, straws, and cups with others and being careful not to kiss anyone on the mouth or face who has an oral cold sore. This is the type of education needed to reduce infection rates. We also need to educate ourselves and our girls about how the infection can be spread through oral and genital contact. Knowing the incubation period of the infection, what the symptoms can be or are most often like, and how to discern if an outbreak is about to occur on the mouth or the genitals are all helpful in reducing the likelihood of spreading the infection.

When my daughter was a senior in high school, she created a questionnaire to evaluate her peers' knowledge of sexually transmitted infections and safe sex practices. The research tool was for a sociology project and randomly distributed in equal numbers through all four grades. Out of 100 total respondents, only 2 answered a question about oral cold sores correctly. Nearly 100 percent were unaware that these cold sores were caused by a herpes virus. Further, they had no idea that this virus could be spread to other people through kissing or oral sex. The sample size was small and the study methodology imperfect, but the questions were well constructed and the answers made it evident how low the level of knowledge is among teens when it comes to herpes and its transmission.

Using condoms and limiting sexual partners is always a good idea and worth reiterating to your teenage daughter. Encouraging teens to really know their partner and avoid one-night stands is the true meaning of safe sex and an important concept to continually reemphasize. In addition, learning as much as you can about the virus and helping your daughter understand it raises everyone's consciousness and tendency to be more careful about who they kiss and when they kiss and about their sexual activity in general.

Contracting HSV I or II is not life-threatening. However, it can shape people's sexual behaviors and choices throughout life, whether they have one partner or several partners.

Whether or not someone with HSV I or II uses anti-viral medication to suppress the virus on a regular basis or just when and if an outbreak occurs depends on many different factors and is beyond the scope of this section. However, resources are available that allow you to stay updated on treatment options and recommendations. Establishing a relationship with a well-educated and experienced health care practitioner is helpful too. References in the back of this book are resources worth utilizing for more detailed information about management of the infection.

Herpes is not curable but it is highly manageable: people can and do live with it and continue to have satisfying sexual lives. Preventing contracting it in the first place is ideal. However, should someone become infected, it shouldn't be seen as a character flaw or a black mark for life, nor is it an unequivocal indicator of sexual promiscuity.

HIV/AIDS, Hepatitis B and C, Gonorrhea, and Syphilis

When parents start to talk about teens having sex and the risks of their contracting a sexually transmitted infection, the first thing out of their mouths is often something like: "Oh my God, she could get AIDS!"

The fact is that while the incidence of HIV/AIDS among teens is on the rise, it is rising in a particular subgroup of the overall teen population. Teens most affected by increasing infection rates of HIV are African American and Hispanic youth. In fact, African Americans account for 55 percent of all HIV-infected youth between the ages of 13 and 24.[13] Furthermore, unless, these teens fall within certain high-risk groups—substance abusers, girls with bisexual male partners, impoverished teens, high school dropouts, teens living on the streets, and/or girls with significantly older male sex partners—routine testing is not generally offered except in pregnancy.

Girls who do not fall into these high-risk groups are not immune to contracting HIV. Infection with HIV, as with all other STIs, is a consequence of behaviors and choices about sexual partners, not of who you inherently are or aren't. This means that all sexually active individuals need to be aware of behaviors that increase their risks of contracting the virus. But, knowing the facts about high-risk behaviors and groups is an important first step in prevention.

Because of the massive awareness and education programs initiated by gay men's health groups and further supported by public health departments, the reality of HIV/AIDS and the need for safe-sex practices have become part of the American dialogue and vernacular when it comes to discussions about preventing the transmission of sexually transmitted infections. However, the specifics of who is at highest risk for contracting HIV have been overlooked in the face of parents' generalized hysteria about whether or not their kids will become infected at all.

The specifics about who is at highest risk for contracting HIV holds true for gonorrhea, syphilis, and hepatitis
B and C. All these infections are communicable, problematic, and highly infectious between sexual partners,
and in some cases life-threatening. However, the majority
of sexually active teens nationwide are not falling into
high-risk groups.

When we talk about sexual activity and teens, let's
keep in mind what is considered normal behavior versus
fringe behavior. If your daughter starts keeping company
with known drug dealers, is using drugs herself, or has a
propensity for gang membership and multiple sex partners, then start worrying big time. Talk with her about
her risks in a no-nonsense manner, and keep your eye on
what she does and where she goes. If, on the other hand,
she's hanging around with kids who are essentially in her
peer group, of a similar socioeconomic class, and displays
serially monogamous tendencies, then return to the start
of this chapter and review the four STIs she's most likely
to contract. Put your concerns about HIV/AIDS on the
back-burner and stop worrying about gonorrhea, syphilis,
and hepatitis B and C too. I am not telling you not to do
a cursory review of these as potential risks. I am saying
that the risks are low and that educating yourself and
your daughter about what is real and *most* likely to be
seen as a complication of her sexual activity is better for
both of you.

When you think of STIs as a risk factor of permanent
standing and you consider the steps necessary to avoid
them, whether they fall into the category of most likely
or least likely, the prevention strategies are nearly identical; condoms are *always* a good idea, with every act of

intercourse, vaginal or anal. Knowing your partner and at least something about their sexual history is at the heart of safe-sex practices; limiting the number of sexual partners lowers your risk of exposure to multiple strains of STIs; and having regular gynecological care that includes routine Pap smears and STI testing if you're sexually active and under 25 is recommended. Last, receiving care from practitioners trained in reproductive health as well as sexually transmitted infection prevention and treatment is invaluable. This may mean a private practitioner, or Planned Parenthood, or a public heath clinic in a major metropolitan area. There is no question that the latter two sites have practitioners who are most accustomed to and up-to-date on screening tests, treatment plans, and interventions for prevention.

Putting a parent at ease about the risks a teenager faces when it comes to sexual activity and STIs isn't easy. Are there risks? Absolutely! Are their ways to avoid them? Most definitely! The most important thing to remember is that the likelihood your daughter will contract an STI is dramatically reduced the more informed you both are about them. She'll benefit from all the useful information you can give her or direct her toward because uninformed sex is much more risky.

At the end of this book there are a number of resources that both you and your daughter can refer to for more in-depth information about everything in this chapter. If you're not a healthcare provider, it's difficult to keep up, and the information can be complicated. Further, new information is coming out all the time regarding transmission issues, new drugs, effective treatments, and prevalence and incidence rates. Current information can help both you and your daughter navigate your way safely through her sexual activity while giving you a realistic view of risk factors.

Talking to girls honestly and openly about their sexual activity is critical to maintaining your role as an authority on the subject, but unless you approach your daughter as her advocate and an ally, she will see you as the enemy, and either launch an assault or retreat entirely. Gently questioning a teenage girl without judgment is an integral part of my evaluation when I am with a teen patient. I ask questions such as "Tell me about your partner, how old is he/she?" or "How do you feel about the relationship you're in and the fact that you're having sex?" Answers to these questions yield significant information about a teenager's opinions and feelings about her sexual activity. There are times when providing good health care for girls means giving them permission to stay involved with their boyfriends or girlfriends, or possibly telling them that it's really okay to say no to an overly assertive partner who may be pressuring them to have sex when they don't really want to.

Comprehensive health care for teens involves soliciting comments about their feelings about sex and combining both good gynecological care with mentoring about sexuality and what's normal. In this case, I am able to establish my role as a safe, reliable authority who can remain objective and instructive, and reassure them that I am *not* the enemy. Ideally, this should be continued and supported by mothers who are more available for backup than I am and who often know their girls best.

When I talk with teenagers about infection prevention and contraception, they are usually all ears and grateful for the information. It's rare that I find myself forcing the content on them or watching their attention wane as I expound on the risks of multiple partners. They also remain interested in how to engage in safe sex and are eager to hear how one can bring up condom use to a boy whose enthusiasm for sex seems unstoppable. Questions like where to buy condoms and whether you have to be 18 are very common. The answers to these questions are factual and once it's clear to me that my patient understands what I have said, then and only then is a discussion of values about sex—hers, not mine—appropriate or potentially helpful. This conversational strategy must apply to mothers talking with daughters as well.

Girls who manage to find their way into my exam room because of their sexual activity are at an advantage over those who never see a health care practitioner. Sometimes, these girls have a big mess on their hands when they arrive. More often, they themselves have made the appointment, knowing they need to prevent a mess from occurring in the first place. Either way, by the time they leave I've made sure they have plenty of information to help prevent or solve problems they might be at risk for. In addition, they have established a relationship with a competent, informed, and caring authority on the subject of sex to whom they can turn for help.

The importance of the alliance between a girl or woman and her ob-gyn practitioner is paramount during a variety of phases in a woman's life. Facilitating a relationship between your daughter and a well-informed, objective, and experienced practitioner is an effective way to help both of you to separate values from facts. It is also an effective way to make a statement about the importance of her overall health and your commitment to it and reinforce your role as a trustworthy authority who can lead her to the help that she needs.

I recently took my 14 year-old to see a nurse-midwife for care. I knew she had been sexually active and although she had been using condoms, I felt that going on birth control pills would be a good idea, in addition to condoms. When we got there, my daughter was shy and not very communicative. I knew she was scared too. It was difficult for the midwife to get the information she needed from her so I decided to help. I told my daughter: "Amanda, you always need to tell this woman everything. She's here to help you and keep you safe." My daughter and I have a pretty good relationship and when she heard me say this she was more able to relax and feel like she could answer the midwife's questions. We both left feeling as though we got the care Amanda needed and had established a relationship with someone who understood her.

— Joan, 44

There are many teens who start off seeing me for their gynecological care as the result of a referral from their pediatrician. At various ages, pediatricians will some-times decide that teens they're seeing are better cared for by women's health care specialists such as midwives. This is especially the case if any reproductive or sexual health issues surface. Jenny was an example of a girl who had been sent to me by her pediatrician who felt that she had reached an impasse with her and that it was time for Jenny to see a specialist.

Jenny was 14 and had been alluding to the fact that she had been sexually active but had never explicitly answered this question when asked by her pediatrician. When she came to see me I made the assumption that she was sexually active. I was also very comfortable talking about sex and Jenny sensed this immediately. It wasn't long into the visit before she told me that she had been having sex with her boyfriend for several months but added: "I haven't been using any birth control." I asked her if her boyfriend ever used condoms, and she told me, "He uses one every time we have sex." I explained to Jenny that condoms were a form of birth control and they also helped prevent people from getting STIs. This was a news flash for her and she was very relieved. We then moved on to my explaining what my exam would involve and when I showed her a speculum and assured her that it was smaller than her boyfriend's penis, she smiled with a look of appreciation on her face that clearly relaxed her and further strengthened the bond that was forming between us as midwife and patient.

By the time our visit was over, Jenny was able to tell me that she was glad she had come and that she felt better knowing the things I had told her. She also promised to come see me again if she needed anything and I told her I would be happy to see her anytime, even if her problem wasn't "down there." She also left with a prescription for and instructions on how to use the hormonal birth control patch for additional contraceptive coverage. She promised to keep using condoms and said she'd call me if she had any more questions. Our visit was a success, by anyone's standards, and I felt my rapport with her would work to her advantage.

Midwives have a tradition of caring for disenfranchised and marginal populations, and teens often fall into these groups. We also seem to be more approach-able for teens because we aren't doctors. Furthermore, our training emphasizes understanding and facilitating normal development and health maintenance across a woman's life span. We do this regardless of our patients' age, socioeconomic, or relational status.

Midwives (and nurse-practitioners) are also known for providing highly personalized care. Ask women of all ages why they see a midwife versus a doctor and they're likely to mention this as a reason. This is significant given the trends in the American health care system, which has depersonalized medicine to an extraordinary degree discouraging patients from getting the very care they need most.

Most midwives, although not all (there are some male midwives), are women and many are mothers. In com-bination with our expertise in reproductive health, this helps us to develop meaningful relationships with our teen patients and their mothers. We understand, from our personal experiences, the importance of mother-child relationships and we are accustomed to and trained in couplet models of care—pregnant women and their fetuses—and a teen and her mother represent an exten-sion and different version of this model. Mothers and daughters benefit when they establish a relationship with a practitioner who specializes in women's health and who believes that health education is a central part of good health care.

Becoming an authority on anything involves study of the subject, patience in implementing your knowledge, and steady and thoughtful management and interven-tion when they're needed. Mothers who can master and embrace this will be promoted to "authority" in their daughters' eyes and are likely to be much more successful in helping them stay safe, happy, and well as they grow from sexually active teens to adult women.

Being an authority on any subject implies a steadiness of demeanor, a capability to manage the unexpected, the knowledge, skill and experience to solve problems, and the ability to triage problems appropriately. Authorities are also confident in their ability to find solutions and can easily distinguish an emergency that requires immediate attention from a problem that can be dealt with in a more leisurely way. This position makes it easier to blend an intelligent response with a caring and compassionate one. This is a wonderful thing to be able to provide your teenage daughter as she finds her way through her sexual identity formation and development.

QUESTIONS TO ASK YOURSELF

Here are some questions to ask yourself about your true position of authority on the subject of teen sexuality. When you ask yourself these questions, see if you already know the answers or not. If the answer is no, it's time to do a little homework before you can hope to compete in your teenager's war against your position as an authority on sex.

- Do I feel truly confident in my knowledge about what STIs my daughter might be at risk for if she is sexually active?

- Am I familiar with how to use a condom correctly and would I be willing to explain this to my daughter?

- Do I know what STIs are curable versus manageable?

- Do I know if you have to be 18 to buy condoms?

- Do I know about all the available birth control methods and which are appropriate for teens?

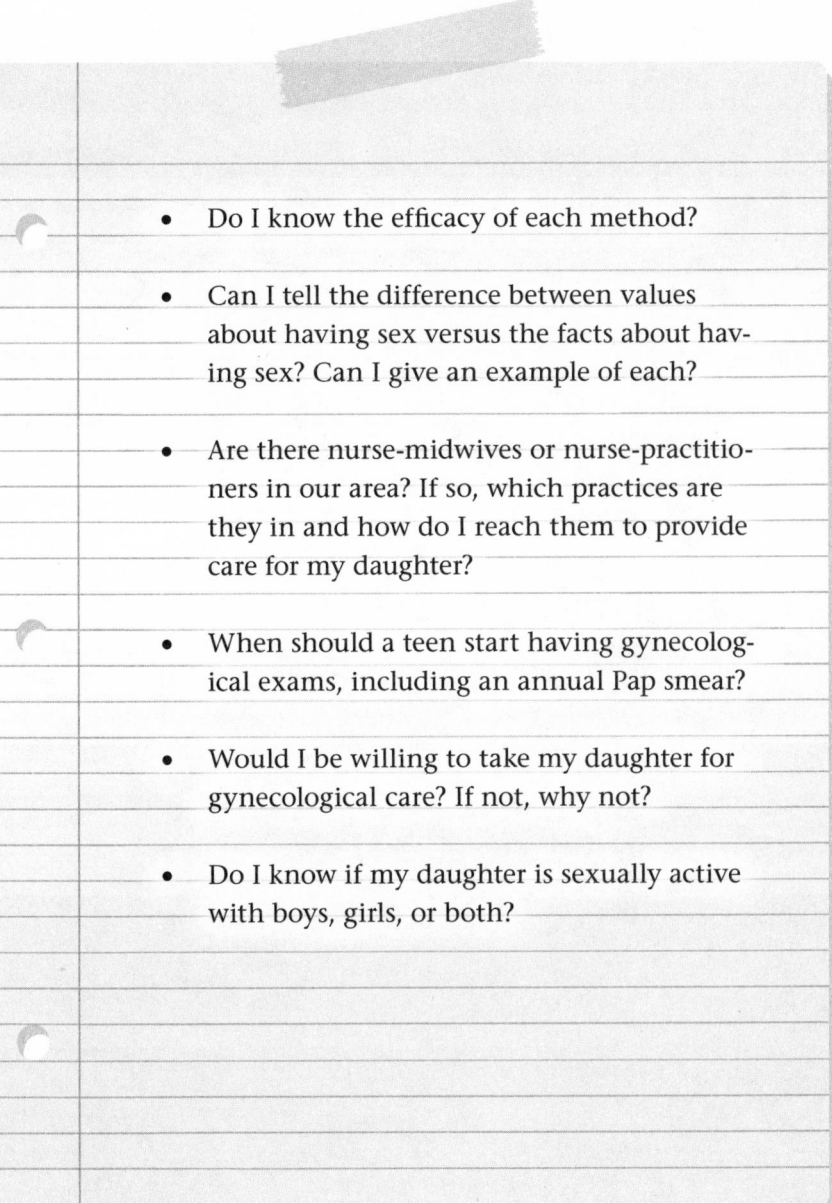

- Do I know the efficacy of each method?

- Can I tell the difference between values about having sex versus the facts about having sex? Can I give an example of each?

- Are there nurse-midwives or nurse-practitioners in our area? If so, which practices are they in and how do I reach them to provide care for my daughter?

- When should a teen start having gynecological exams, including an annual Pap smear?

- Would I be willing to take my daughter for gynecological care? If not, why not?

- Do I know if my daughter is sexually active with boys, girls, or both?

CHAPTER 5

THE CLOSED CULTURE OF COOL

"Each friend represents a world in us,
a world possibly not born until they arrive, and it is
only by this meeting that a new world is born."

— Anaïs Nin

It's a hard pill to swallow, but the fact is if you're parenting a teenage girl you will one day be conscripted to the ranks of least appealing, least smart, least funny, least interesting, and definitely the least cool person who ever lived. Prepare yourself. This will last for several years. In one of my own trying moments as a parent, when my daughter was 17, I was so incredibly uncool and lacking in intelligence that she told me she couldn't understand how I managed to stay employed! It was one of those moments in my daughter's adolescence that I will never forget. The comment was hurtful yet so utterly preposterous that laughter was the only reasonable response. Laughter is really your best defense and in battles like these; humor should always win out. In our case it did, and she and I still joke about that ridiculous moment now.

Being cool is a huge part of the teen experience, and it starts long before adolescence. What drives it is the desire to feel accepted as a member of an identifiable community. Enter teen peer group, exit parents, especially mothers. For teenage girls, mothers are often particularly uncool while fathers run a close second. No doubt this is connected to the drive to individuate and insure that you're anything *but* your mother.

Family life and its participants at this phase of development should ideally provide a backdrop for community, a safety net of sorts. Teens need to know their families are there should they require something that their peer group can't provide. And, more important, family, at its best, maintains a scaffold of civility and social organization so that when teenagers get a little wild, parents can step in and corral the beast. However, teens' peers remain in the foreground of their social lives. And, as a bonus, the families of their friends give your girls an opportunity to observe how other families operate, and to decide what they like about their own family and what they don't.

The offense that many parents take when their girls decide not to participate in their own family's activities often elicits a disproportionately negative response, especially from mothers. This is unreasonable, and, to be frank, as far as your daughter is concerned, a big part of what makes you so incredibly uncool. This is a time when we mothers simply have to step aside and tough it out. Your girl is already very familiar with her own family's traditions and ideas of having fun. What she's looking for is new data and a real break from all she knows best. So give it to her.

Moreover, when she does have this information, don't be surprised when she reports it back to you and her stories include editorial comments about how cool it is in comparison to what her own family does. Ouch! At these stinging moments, it's helpful to remember that this is a necessary phase in her journey toward independence. Our responsibility is to simply endure it, knowing it will eventually pass and assume a more normal place in her social interactions. But for now, you must be resigned to being closed out of your daughter's culture of cool, until such time as she is ready to let you back in.

The early teen years are often the most turbulent and trying, and although I had had plenty of experience working with teens, having my own teenager was very different. Even the most experienced, patient, and dedicated parents can face challenges with their girls that leave them feeling exhausted and sometimes desperate for relief from the stress of living with an adored child who is making life difficult for everyone—especially her mother. If you should find yourself in this situation and you feel that you're at the end of your rope, out of patience and ideas to manage, don't be afraid to ask for help from mental health providers, school counselors, and your child's teacher. And, don't be afraid to admit that you need a break from your daughter.

In my case, this was absolutely true; when Thalia was 13, she and I were often at each other's throats. Our household and our interactions were tumultuous. It was like living in a minefield; there was always the possibility of stepping on a bomb you didn't even realize was underfoot and having it explode. Finally, my daughter asked if she could live with my sister-in-law and her family in Florida. She wanted something completely different. At first, I was all for it, and in fact I said, "Sure," with a kind of glee. In retrospect, I realize what I was feeling in that moment was an easy escape for immediate relief, a way out of the frequent fighting and exhausting disagreements over virtually nothing of real significance. I also was familiar and comfortable with this model; I myself had gone to boarding school in my freshman year of high school and still believe it was the best thing I could have done at the time.

A few days after I had so easily consented, the reality that my daughter would be packing her bags and leaving for the year was heartbreaking. But it was too late. I had made the agreement and plans were already in place.

Thalia's tenure in Florida did not prove to be the geographic and new family cure that she had quite imagined. She brought her turbulent young teen self right along with her suitcase. She had the same young-teen-girl problems in Florida she had been having in Massachusetts. To my sister-in-law's credit she hung in there with my daughter and her three kids, making the best of things and allowing my daughter to experience the natural consequences of her behavior in Florida as I had tried to 1,300 miles north. The ten months apart gave Thalia and me a break from each other, and when she returned to New England for her sophomore year in high school, she was more mature, less volatile, and more appreciative of what her life with her immediate family was all about. I had recovered from the battles of the previous year, was calmer, wiser, and happy to have her home.

When I look back on that year and my experience of letting her go, I realize it was the best thing that could have happened at the time. It was genuinely therapeutic for me and it informed Thalia about her behavior, preferences, and place in a world much bigger than her family.

In our case, letting go more than one might imagine doing at such a time meant getting back what we both needed and wanted: more of each other's essence. It was a great place to start over.

If you don't have a family member that can take your daughter in for a year like I did and boarding school isn't an affordable option, then look for other ways that the two of you can have regular time apart. I used to announce that I was off-duty at 8:00 P.M. If my daughter had any questions, requests, or complaints to register, she needed it to do so before my time clock went off. This was a great way to ensure that I had peace, quiet, and some distance from her in the evenings. You may also be able to work something out one or two days per week or on weekends with the family one of her friends and offer the same in return. Summer programs are also a great idea, especially if your daughter can work as well as participate in the program she's attending. Living with a young teen girl whose moods are labile and who may consider you her stupid slave most of the time requires an enormous amount of effort and stamina. If you're a normal woman and especially if you work outside the home and live with and face stressors like the rest of us, it may feel sometimes that your daughter is trying to kill you. Under such circumstances, regularly scheduled breaks are your best bet for survival. And don't necessarily expect that she'll participate willingly in this plan. You may simply need to tell her that the plan is in place and she has no choice about it. Should she protest tell her it's a matter of life and death—yours and hers!

Communication between human beings is a complex system of subtle and often unconscious cues and patterns. As newborns, we begin our tutorial in human communication by observing the captivating and engaging faces of our mothers. It is a mother's loving smile, soft and undulating voice, and enveloping expressions that babies see with frequency which give them information about the meaning of facial expressions and the importance of body language. Infants are great flirts and it's through their flirtatious behavior that they begin to learn the subtleties and nuances of human communication.[1]

As we become well acquainted with variations in the fabric of the human face, we respond with matching subtlety or overt expressions, often without giving it a second thought. Our fluency in expression and interpretation expands by leaps and bounds. And as we grow and mature, the complexity of our patterns increases without our even knowing it.

When people are mentally healthy, their emotional experiences, sentiments, and thoughts can be expressed more comprehensively to others. Sometimes, people's connections will propel conversations to continue. As they recognize similarities between themselves, their attachment will grow and strengthen. This is particularly true in teens whose limbic brain function is dominant. In a group of teens, all of whom are firing simultaneously on the same wavelength, sharing pitch, cadence, content, and sentiment, imagine the sense of belonging this engenders to the participants in the group! The simple truth is we parents cannot possibly share this with our kids in the ways their friends can—nor should we try.

Mom tells me all the time that me and my friends sound alike. She says that we all sound like Valley Girls and that our speech is fake. I don't know what she's talking about. We have our own voices and I don't think we sound the same. We're just friends that hang out together, that's all.

— Tina, 15

No matter how bizarre your daughter's speech and communication patterns may seem to you, they are merely emblematic of her group membership. Tattoos, piercings, similar clothing styles, and common interests can be like this too. These shared traits and features are like secret decoder rings that you only get once you become an initiate into a group. Becoming a member of a recognized group holds immeasurable magnetism, clout, and sense of security for teens.

Bravado, especially when it comes to sexual exploits, can redefine a teen in a matter of one afternoon or evening. A girl's status within a pack can change overnight from veritable newbie to Queen Bee. Do something, anything, extraordinary and you're the girl in the know. Suddenly other group members are emulating you. This couldn't be more the case than when it comes to sexuality and the commencement of sexual activity, sexual expression, or dating a desirable catch. The fact is, to your daughter, this may be the height of coolness.

The need to seek ultimate coolness is understandable but it can be accompanied by high-risk behaviors that can lead kids into serious messes. There are times when being as cool as you can be involves drugs and alcohol, and there's no question that this can lead to problematic and sometimes life-threatening consequences. Other than hoping for the best, parents can and should step up and prepare kids by talking to them repeatedly about the risks of drug and alcohol use. They also need to familiarize themselves with signs and symptoms of substance use and look out for evidence of it happening in the moment.

The small town we live in has its share of teenage drug and alcohol abusers. In fact, we may actually have more than our share. Western Massachusetts happens to be relatively close to New York City and so we have plenty of drug trafficking with carriers en route from Manhattan to cities and towns throughout New England. It wasn't uncommon when I was on call for our local hospital for me to deliver a young woman in the emergency room whose crack cocaine use had triggered premature labor. These preterm moms were generally "in the business" and had just done a bit too much of the stuff, thus activating the onset of labor ahead of schedule.

Knowing this, I was always on the lookout for their wares being peddled 25 miles south of the main drug corridor, on the streets of our hometown and where my daughter was in high school. Marijuana, heroin, cocaine, and crack were easily purchased, and this became more evident as she went through high school. In fact, in the three years my daughter attended our local high school, there were some impressive drug busts in our otherwise sleepy arts and culture community, and they were all the buzz. Between the four of us—our two kids, my partner, and me—we each knew at least one person who had been arrested.

Having created my own version of a James Dean persona as a teen and having a spouse who could sniff out a lie before it had been completely spoken gave me the advantage of an honest-to-goodness heads-up when it came to tracking down this behavior in my own teen. I am happy to say there wasn't too much of it. However, I was well aware of the potential risks and made a point of talking about them until the cows came home and my daughter was on the verge of slugging me.

I *always* asked who the designated driver was and I made sure that when kids left my house, they all knew I was the parent to call if something changed with the original plan or went wrong. This meant staying by my land line or keeping my cell phone with me if I went out. I insisted on hearing by 11:00 P.M. what the plan was for the rest of the evening. If no one had shown up by then, I would expect a call and being told, honestly, where everyone was going to be for the night. And I talked on and on about the risks of being stoned or drunk and running up against unsolicited sexual advances. I stressed how this could lead to nothing but regret and problems of significant magnitude. This was especially important with my girl, who had numerous suitors and was not only a stunner but also had an intriguing and highly appealing "Xena, Warrior Princess" personality. I included every current statistic about roofies I could find and repeated the importance of not drinking out of cups handed to you by a stranger or even a friend. It got to the point that I could have probably said these things in my sleep. However, each time I recited my litany of precautionary measures, I made sure to change the inflection in my voice enough and use enough words from my internal thesaurus to grab the attention of all teens present. Sometimes I blocked the door and didn't let them leave until I was finished.

Snagging and hanging on to the attention of a group of teens about to head out to party is like herding cats. And I knew that despite my efforts I was sure to find evidence that my warnings went unheeded from time to time. Because of this, I wasn't at all surprised when I found a fifth of vodka in the family freezer on prom night. Somehow she had managed to procure this illegal refreshment and put it on ice so that it would be well chilled for the after-prom festivities. I poured it down the drain, of course, and when she went to retrieve it while her friends waited in the car outside, she was hopping mad to find it missing. Knowing perfectly well what had happened, she came at me with both barrels loaded, complaining about how expensive it had been and that I had wasted her money. Oh, I was all torn up! As I put it: "Gee, it's a bummer being you tonight." I figured it was the least I could do to help insure her safety on a night that is notoriously troublesome if not downright lethal for teens across the country. In the end, she sought comfort from her sympathetic pack—after all, that's what they're there for.

The Guttmacher Institute, an organization that studies reproductive health, reports that 46 percent of teens ages 15–19 have indicated that they have had sexual intercourse at least once. Further, more than three quarters of the girls who reported being sexually active stated that their first sexual experience was with a steady boyfriend, fiancé, or cohabiting partner. From my experience as a midwife, I know that teens don't always admit to having sex so it's likely that these rates are lower than the actual numbers. At any rate, this statistic reflects just how normal it is for teens to be sexually active.[2]

Our culture emphasizes and encourages coupling. This is no surprise for a species that thrives in packs. Those of us who are happily coupled feel terribly sorry for our friends who are single and "all by themselves." Those of us who are less than happily coupled may envy them to varying degrees, but nonetheless often choose to stay in our less than happy relationships rather than face life without a partner.

Parents of teens make the mistake of thinking that the advantages of being coupled aren't significant until after the teen years have passed. As parents, we often assume we fill this role of quasi-partner, and until our daughters grow up and marry, the family should be enough to satisfy their needs for socializing and emotional closeness. First of all, it doesn't feel this way to your daughter. And second, if you are acting this way or parenting in this fashion, stop it right now! You are putting your daughter in danger of being labeled as "uncool" and interfering with her ability to achieve status and recognition in her peer group, not to mention her ability to form independent and loving relationships with people her own age. You're not her friend, you're her parent, and it's important that you stay in that role for the sake of her safety and healthy development.

I often hear from mothers of teens that all their daughters want to do is hang out with friends or significant other. Yes, so what else is new? When my daughter and her first long-term love were at our house, we never saw them. In fact, I wasn't even sure they were in her room and I would knock occasionally, wondering if anyone would answer.

One evening when dinner was nearly on the table, I called out in my most cheerful voice: "Hey, you two lovebirds, dinner is on the table. Come and join us." The answer I got was: "No thanks, we're not hungry." In the words of Barry White, master of love, these two had all they needed. They were thriving on each other's company and their being able to do so safely in our home made me feel honored. Despite the fact that I barely saw any real evidence of their existence, I knew where they were, that they were safe, and that they were acting like normal teenagers in love.

Teenagers usually don't want their mom or dad to be the one to go out to dinner with them when they want company or hang out with them when they're working on a project for school. If your teen daughter declares otherwise, then this is a different story. You will get this request once in a while, when she has an occasional setback of her chronological development and acts younger than her actual age. Generally speaking, though, being the mother of a teenage daughter demands what can feel like an inordinate amount of patience and carefully maintained space. You might want to do all those things with your girl because you love and miss her, but if she's not interested in spending time with you, you just have to wait it out until she is. You also have to force yourself to stop being "helpful." The more she takes responsibility for her own laundry, making her lunches, and arranging her ride to the dance on Saturday, the more competent she will become.

In my own experience, having dinner, a relaxed chat, or joint television viewing with my daughter comes about once a week. I leave it up to her to initiate it and when she does, I'm right there, even if it means changing my own plans.

I can't always make heads or tails out of my daughter's interest in spending time with me. Chances are, she's not premenstrual, isn't feeling too strained by thoughts of her future, has had a good day in school, and hasn't had any major tiffs with her friends or boyfriend; all good news for both of us. It means I get an infusion of my daughter's company and she gets what I hope remains an inoculating dose of maternal love, attention, reassurance, and support for simply being who she is, regardless of her failings, flaws, or stellar attributes. I get another opportunity to remind myself that she does have a sweet side despite what can often feel like a mountain of evidence to the contrary, and she gets a chance to record in her data bank that she has a truly loving mother who would take a bullet for her any day.

This one night a week leaves a lot of other time when my daughter and I are not together. But she's a teenager and this is what she's supposed to be doing—finding important relationships outside of the home, building networks, and honing relationship skills that will sustain her in her adult life. Just ask yourself: when you are not with your daughter, who are you likely to be with? If you have a beloved in your life and it's a healthy and loving relationship, the answer is that you are probably with your sweetheart. Now ask yourself another question: when your daughter isn't with you, who is she likely to be with? The answer may be her current love, that person in her life whom she enjoys being with most of all.

Chances are, she wants exactly what you want—loving companionship and the neurochemical bliss that it brings. When you really analyze her behavior, the secret culture of cool does not seem to be as secret as you might have thought.

Friends and an active romantic relationship make your girl feel like she belongs somewhere other than at home, and that her thoughts, opinions, and presence matter to someone other than her parents. This is especially important given that she doesn't naturally feel that she belongs with you at this phase of life anyway. In fact, the time you have to worry is if your daughter doesn't have a peer group or a sweetheart. If your daughter spends all her free time with you, alone, or on a computer, pay close attention. It can be an indication that things are not going well in her life. Isolationists and loners, who remain unattached to any peers in their age group, run the risk of becoming dangerously alienated, depressed, and antisocial.

Being a midwife and caring for so many teens has necessitated the development of rapid, on-the-spot assessment skills of all body systems simultaneously. This has become especially true in this day and age of shortened medical appointments. I know these are very difficult on patients who need more than ten minutes. But, just for the record, they're hard on practitioners too. We often don't have all the time we would ideally like to talk with patients in a way we know is ideal. In order to cope with today's facts of health care practice, those of us still in the business have had to really hone our assessment skills in order to accomplish many things simultaneously. One of the ways I do this is by watching and looking closely (and inconspicuously) at my patients when I am talking to them in the exam room or my office. Posture, skin tone, hairstyles and clothing, hygiene, and willingness to communicate speak volumes about someone's state of mind.

Teen girls who are barely conversant, answer in monosyllables or three-word sentences, aren't dressed in some version of the latest clothing styles, aren't clean and tidy, and sit with their shoulder slumped are shining a neon sign in my face that reads: "I am depressed, hate myself, have no friends. *Help!*" These are visits that demand moving through my physical exam quickly to save time for a psychological assessment.

Betsy was a 17-year-old who came to me for crippling menstrual cramps and migraines. She was missing school at least one week out of the month because she was home with pain. When I took one look at her, I realized that whatever migraine headaches and cramping she was having, there was something else going on with this kid that was much more serious.

Betsy was a bit overweight, had terrible acne, was not stylish in any way, and was very withdrawn. She had come with her mother to this visit, not altogether typical for a 17-year-old girl. At this point in adolescence, most girls drive themselves to their appointments and don't want their mother anywhere near my office. I did an exam and we discussed ways that we could manage her cramps, acne, and maybe even her migraines with birth control pills. She was fine with this idea and I told her I would give her a prescription at the end of our visit. With my exam and a management plan of her chief complaints behind me, I started asking her questions about her life and how things were going in school, with friends, and with her family. That's when I hit paydirt. I quickly discovered that this girl's demeanor and physical presentation represented a state of mind that I had suspected; she was miserably depressed and at very high risk for suicide. Betsy didn't come right out and say these things exactly, but what she did tell me and the way she described her feelings and daily life were very revealing. And she had been experiencing these feelings for most of her adolescence, and no one seemed to notice!

Betsy was a straight-A student and headed toward a great college but had no real friends to speak of. She was teased at school about her acne, weight, and general demeanor. She was a loner out of necessity as she didn't feel safe around her peers should they ask her to join them. Her parents were very serious, and worked as professors at a local, highly competitive, private New England college in our area. They had missed every sign that their daughter's teenage life was not normal, nor was her behavior. In their opinion, her studiousness and avoidance of social activity was to be commended and encouraged and portended a bright academic future and scholarly position—just like theirs. Meanwhile, while I listened to Betsy's answers to my questions I imagined her looking at which nearby tree would be strong enough and secluded enough for her to successfully string up a rope, throw it around her neck, and knock out the stool from underneath her feet. Macabre humor aside, depression is serious business and clinical depression has a high lethality rate when it remains untreated over long periods of time. It's also not that uncommon in teens.

I just asked one simple question: "Betsy, you seem really sad to me. Is this true?" The dam burst and the poor kid was sobbing in my office. Never mind her menstrual cramps, migraines, and acne. These were the least of her problems. Fortunately, though, they were enough of a problem that they brought her in for care with me— Hallelujah! Betsy's mother hadn't been in the room during her exam or our conversation about her mood. Now was the time to have her join us, so with Betsy's permission, I called her in from the reception area.

When she arrived and saw her daughter's lack of composure and tear-stained face, I know she was stunned and wondering what I had done to her. I explained what happened and, in a very sympathetic but commanding voice, told them that Betsy's state of mind was dangerously fragile and that mental health care was absolutely necessary.

Betsy's mother had absolutely no clue what I was talking about. As far as she was concerned, Betsy was doing fine. In fact, she told me that it was her hell-raising, average grades, and "popular girl" sister who was the problem for the family. After all, Betsy was a well above average student and never did anything that made anyone angry or worried. I hated to be the one to break it to her, but so be it; I made it abundantly clear that while Betsy's sister may very well be a pain in the rear, she was acting like a normal teen and that the mother's attention needed to be redirected—like a laser beam—on Betsy. Never mind her other daughter at the moment, and as a matter of fact leaving her alone for a while might be the best idea for everyone as the extra attention her bad behavior was garnering wasn't necessary or helpful.

By the time they left my office, Betsy had a prescription for birth control pills to treat her menstrual cramps and hopefully improve her acne and migraines. I also explained to both Betsy and her mother that the first place to start making a dent in her mood was by improving her sleep, which she said had been terrible for quite a while. Apparently, she had difficulty falling asleep and woke up in the middle of the night worrying about all sorts of things.

I gave her mother a small supply of medication for Betsy to take an hour before she went to bed to help her get her sleep cycle back on track and reduce the anxiety she had described. I also referred them to an adolescent psychiatrist in our area and encouraged them to make an appointment as soon as possible. I explained that Betsy needed a more comprehensive visit with her to see whether or not an antidepressant was indicated. I also asked Betsy to promise me that she wouldn't do anything to harm herself and if she felt she was going to, that she would come in to see me immediately. I also suggested they make an appointment with a family therapist who could work with the adults in this family and help them gain insight into what was normal and abnormal teen behavior and help them parent with greater awareness and therefore be more effective. No doubt Betsy's sister had been taking a real beating as a constant comparison to Betsy and needed as much support as Betsy did.

The parents of these two girls needed much more information about the culture and importance of being cool, having a peer group, and being rebellious when you're a teenager. Betsy wasn't likely to have a place among her sister's friends, but she needed help and support to find other teens more like her and create a place for herself within a group of like-minded people her age. Given her high intellect and academic prowess, maybe she would flourish the math club or debate team. There had to be something more sociable and interesting that would give her time to build friendships and provide a counterbalance to the pressure to succeed that she felt dominated her life and relationship with her parents. Her parents were certainly well meaning and very concerned about Betsy when I brought her symptoms to their attention. The fact was that they simply had no real understanding of the combination of markers of emotional well-being that indicate sound general health in teenage girls—friendships being a primary one.

Girlfriends often make up a teenage girl's primary and dominant social network as she progresses through adolescence. As girls mature and migrate away from family they become more focused on friends for companionship, emotional support and, for better and worse, advice. It is not uncommon for teenage girls to identify each other as the people they feel closest to and most interested in. Girlfriends in adolescence provide unparalleled opportunities for growth and advancement of self. They also teach each other how to behave in a group.

The relational orientation of girls has been studied in depth by a variety of social scientists, educators, and psychologists. Girls are naturally relational beings, relying on one another for interaction, reflection, and the pure pleasure of socialization. Although they often have a best friend, girls also cultivate, develop, and sustain many collateral relationships more easily and naturally than boys do.[3]

Friendships are jewels to many girls—highly valued and deeply treasured. Beginning with sleepovers and advancing to weekend getaways in adulthood, girls (and later women) describe a dependency on and attachment to their girlfriends that contributes to their emotional stability and their overall contentment throughout their entire lives.

My own daughter went through a period in middle school and early high school when her friendships with girls were troublesome, sometimes cruel and very limited. Once this passed, she openly expressed her relief and was able to articulate the sadness she had felt when she was without a best girlfriend and a group of girls that she could identify as peers.

Emotional support, companionship, and fun aren't the only things girls seek from their relationships with each other. They also extend and receive physical affection and are able to enjoy the pleasure of this while reaping the benefits of advancing their social skills through touching and being touched.

Our culture has supported and fostered the development of sensuality in girls much more so than in boys. Relational games like playing house, an interest in fine motor skill activities like knitting and sewing versus the gross motor movements of "real boys," music, art projects and cooking are examples of the gender-specific activities that we associate with girls and encourage them to engage in together. These ideas and implicit behavioral expectations can be confining in some ways but they also come with freedom to be more demonstrative and loving in ways we don't extend to boys. It's not uncommon nor thought of as odd for girls to walk arm in arm, share the same bed when sleeping over, shower together, or brush one another's hair. This is rarely the case for boys in this country.

Teen girls adapt and devise friendships to fit the needs and concerns of their teen life. This is why a best friend from grade school may end up a thing of the past once high school starts. In adolescence, your daughter's girlfriends can easily become her alternate family and often feel to her as if they're meeting her most pressing needs for communion with like-minded souls. They also are simply more fun than her family of origin could possibly be at a time when the differences between her and her family seem glaring to her. Paying attention to how your daughter relates to her girlfriends and manages the inevitable upsets and disturbances that arise in these groups can give you good information about how she's faring overall.

Sad but true: teen girls are masters of emotional excess. The increases in estrogen and progesterone alone make them more sensitive to physical and emotional pain.[4] They can be positively intense when their limbic brains, combined with their fluctuating hormones, detect what they perceive as a threat or disturbance in their environment, and that includes disruptions and perceived injustices in their friendships. Honestly, you'd think the world was coming to an end sometimes the way they can carry on. Because of this emotional fervor and because mothers often feel so desperate to connect when their girls start moving away from them and toward other girls, it's easy for even the most astute mother to be yanked by her figurative collar into her daughter's emotional excess, and to take sides with her, and against her friends in any given teen tragedy. Take my advice; beware of this inclination to get too involved! You will pay for it down the line!

Mom is way too involved with me and my friends. She asks too many questions and it seems like she sort of tries to be one of us when she talks to me about what's going on with us. It's kind of annoying and it makes me feel uncomfortable. I know she's trying to be helpful, but, it's really not helpful at all. I wish she'd just stay out of my business with my friends. I can solve my own problems when they come up and she's too old to really understand what's going on anyway. I just want her to be my mom, not my friend.

— Jessica, 14

The experience of our daughters delving deeper into their relationships with their friends and farther away from us can feel like a wind chill factor of 20 below. This is a time to strive for a binocular view, not a microscopic one. You'll still feel the chilly winds but they won't hit you with the same force if you stay on the sidelines, involved from a distance.

Continue to offer your presence, but refrain from extending your involvement unless you have real reasons to suspect that things aren't going well. More often than not, the best contribution you can make is the frequent repetition of the commandments of good friendship: honesty, support, integrity, and kindness. And continue setting an example of this in real life by maintaining meaningful and healthy friendships with other women.

Frankly, the extent to which girls help each other out sometimes is nothing short of extraordinary. This mutual aid and support often reflects an understanding of the fact that many girls are having difficulty relying on their parents, especially mothers, for support and advocacy during their teens. Even girls who don't necessarily like one another all that much will extend a helping hand if they sense that someone is really in trouble, and can't reach out to her parents for one reason or another.

Despite the fact that girls can dump one another in a flash over things we adults find astoundingly insignificant, they will also provide a sling and hammock for one another to fall into when trouble looms. This is especially true when sexual crises and safety issues are involved. I have had plenty of teen girls show up at my office with their best friend when they need contraception or are worried about being pregnant.

I looked at my schedule one day at work and noticed that I was starting my morning with Andrea, a 16-year-old. I thought this was odd as most kids this age are in school at this hour. Something was obviously wrong for her to skip school and come to see me at 9:00 A.M.

When I entered the exam room, Andrea was sitting on the exam table and two friends were sitting in chairs. Wow, a regular girls' party. My assistant then knocked on the door and asked to speak to me for a moment. You could feel the tension soar in the room. I walked out and was informed that Andrea had come in with a question of pregnancy and in fact her pregnancy test was positive. No wonder the teen contingent. Usually, by this time, girls themselves have already bought an early pregnancy test from a pharmacy and come to me hoping that my pregnancy tests and skills are more magically right and that they'll find out that there's been an error and they're not pregnant at all.

I sat down, sighed, and said, "So, bummer. You're pregnant." Simultaneously, like synchronized swimmers, all three of them gasped, and then Andrea burst into tears. Like ladies in waiting in Elizabeth's court, the other two came running to her side as if preparing for her to faint. Despite the fact that all three had been aware of this already, the shock of my saying it was simply more than they could manage separately. They needed to physically stick together to withstand the blow. It was fascinating.

Needless to say, this wasn't what they were hoping for. Andrea had a serious day ahead of her. She would have to go to her mother, tell her she was pregnant, and then make a decision about a plan. Once this was established, as if I wasn't even in the room, the three of them moved into a conversation that involved plans to maintain contact with one another throughout the process of disclosure and provide Andrea with the comfort of girlfriends close by. By this time, they really didn't need me and I ended our visit by telling her to contact me anytime if I could be of anymore help to her.

Girls can be very generous with each other when they need to be. Perhaps this is because girls know, better than anyone, just how dangerous and difficult being a teen can be, especially if your mother is not available or a "psycho mom" who is likely to completely overreact to even the smallest infractions.

Sometimes the help girls give one another can mean the difference between life and death. The teen who told me the story below gave me clear information about how and why this happens between girls.

There was a party that we all went to and I was the designated driver. I don't drink beer and getting wasted just doesn't feel so cool to me. Anyway, there was some tequila that was there— really good quality—that was passed around for people to try. Stuff that was expensive, you know, not the kind of stuff that you just get wasted on. Anyway, one of my friends got really drunk and then started to vomit all over the place. She's done this before and it's a drag to deal with her, but I like her, and anyway, her mother is a total psycho and I didn't want her to get in trouble. So, I/we dealt with it and got her home. It was late so even though her mother was there, she didn't know what was going on. I hate the fact that she's done this so many times, but I wasn't going to leave her there or let her drive home.

— Tanya, 17

Some may read this and consider it aiding and abetting, but teens are working with different laws. They see this as necessary and justifiable help and in this case it was truly a life-saving intervention. Whether or not the girl who was helped has a drinking problem or not is beyond the scope of this chapter. The point here is the sense of devotion and recognition that something was wrong and potentially life-threatening and if a mother couldn't help someone else needed to step up to the plate. Teen girls will do this for each other.

The support and guidance girls give each other is a great thing and we should all be grateful for it. But there's another side to the coin of girls' friendships—and it's not pretty.

Gossip, competition for and with one another, out-and-out lying about what was said or done, and exclusion from groups are not uncommon behaviors in girls' relationships with one another. Sometimes the cruelty that's displayed has a ferocity and lifespan that can be extremely stressful and difficult to untangle. The fighting can get ugly. Real meanness and unrelenting emotional torture tend to be much more likely in younger teens. Just ask any girl in middle school.

Depending on the temperament of your girl and the persistence of her torturers, the teasing and gossip can become unbearable. Your daughter may come home in tears every day after school, withdraw from social contact, and feel miserably depressed. However, each girl, including your own, can play a role in a friendship that has gone to the dogs and it's important to take an aerial view when it comes to the reports she's bringing home to you.

It's hard to imagine that your own daughter may be a perpetrator of bullying especially if she is telling you about being tortured by others. But even the most passive girls can hunt their prey down and deliver a verbal insult with shocking force. In fact, girls who have been tormented by bullies themselves are actually more likely to bully others.[5] Sad but true. The reason they do this comes from their fear and anxiety of being an outsider and their desperate need for group membership and identification. It's never a bad idea, once the report of her causalities is over, to look at your daughter with sincerity and ask: "How and why do you think you got to this point with your friends?" When you're listening to her answer, pay attention to whether or not she includes herself in any way as possibly having contributed to the origins of the conflict. If she leaves herself out of it completely, you need to remind her that everyone plays a role in these kinds of things, even if it's a passive one.

In contemporary culture we have a new forum for attack and meanness that didn't exist when I was a teenager: online social networking sites. This virtual world has become quite the stage for bad behavior that often goes unnoticed or completely forgotten by less tech-savvy parents who simply forget about this virtual reality. If your girl has a page on one of these sites, make a point of checking it regularly and seriously acquaint yourself with what's there and who's on her friends list. Talk with her about what she posts and why and alert her to the fact that the anonymity of the Internet has its benefits and disadvantages. This can include encouraging a bizarre and inconsiderate bravado on the part of meanies out there who can taunt and torture their victims with no real sense of the consequences.

All relationships are dynamic and although the balance may be tipped in someone else's favor, teaching your daughter skills to manage heartless teasing without losing her sense of self-worth is critically important. If the rifts and exclusion are repetitive and cruel enough that she is becoming depressed, you may have to consider addressing the topic of bullying with her school administrators, seeking mental health counseling for support, or even changing schools.

Actively listening to her experience, acknowledging her feelings, and expressing your sorrow that she's going through this are critical in helping her manage and feel she has a safe haven at home. As far as your instruction and advice, keep in mind that your goal is to fortify a strong sense of self and the right to her feelings. The stronger her sense of self and self-worth is, the less likely it will be that her friends' behaviors, in general and toward her, will influence her when it comes to making decisions—including decisions about being sexually active or not and with whom.

The shifting, bifurcation, and splitting that goes on in packs of girls is somewhat unavoidable. In this mass of forming personalities is the simultaneous development of everyone's sexual identity. Sometimes, sexual identity formation is an integral aspect in their choice of friends.

To some extent, all girls will develop friendships with a variety of girls. Some will be pleasing to you, others will seem like odd and enigmatic choices and, of course, others will be frankly untenable. Keep in mind that girls need to develop a unique identity, and this includes choosing a variety of friends, some of whom might be quite different from your daughter. It's a part of the experimentation that goes into the creation of self. It's a bit like trying on new and different outfits you've never imagined yourself wearing. However, this is a time to pay close attention from a distance to how your daughter is behaving, and who she is spending her time with.

If she is hanging out with fast girls and showing atypical bravado, unless it's downright disrespectful or dangerous, let her live in it and see what happens. Bravado may be obnoxious, but it's not necessarily bad or indicative of increasing risk or danger. On the other hand, if she's becoming a changeling and you barely recognize who she is anymore, then you must address it in ways that will lend credence to your observation and opinion. It's not a crime to point out how different your daughter seems since she's been hanging out with her new friends, and you can do this without preaching. Simply articulating your observations without drama in your voice can be thought-provoking for her and not leave her feeling threatened and embarrassed. And don't worry, just because your daughter is trying out different friends doesn't necessarily mean that this is who and what she will become. In teenagers, birds of a feather do not necessarily flock together.

Mothers worry that girlfriends will sway their daughter to become sexually active. Whether or not this is actually a risk for your daughter is likely to have more to do with the sturdiness of her sense of self than her friends talking her into something she's really not ready for or interested in.

Think about what kind of person your daughter is. Has she always had a mind of her own or is she a follower? Has she always been a kid who loved sensual things like clothes, soft toys, animals, or dancing to her favorite music? Did she masturbate from an early age and seem very sexually awake? What has her confidence level been throughout her life? Is she shy or outgoing? These factors will likely influence her decision to have sex with someone far more than a friend might.

If you're a mother who has negative feelings about your daughter being sexually active as a teen, it's much easier to blame the commencement of this activity on her friends than it is to see this as something she herself has sought out. This may prove to be a time you have to come face-to-face with an aspect of your daughter as an individual that can prove extraordinarily difficult for you. If your daughter has a friend or friends that you know are sexually active and you're wondering whether or not they've influenced her in any way, you might want to consider simply asking her. Then reassure her that if she is having sex with someone, you want to know so that you can make sure that she has everything she needs to keep her safe. By asking her in this way, you're making an assumption that can let her off an uncomfortable hook and the result may very well be a much more honest answer than it would have been otherwise. Asking her in this direct way also takes her off the defensive when it comes to her friendships, which she will fight you on should she feel their status is being challenged or threatened.

Presto—you've just killed two birds with one stone!

You don't have to be a genius, spy, or psychic to figure out with reasonable certainty whether or not one of your daughter's peers is sexually active. You also probably know intuitively whether or not your daughter is. From my personal and professional experience, I have found that girls' physical and often emotional maturation seems to accelerate once they commence their sexual activity. They look and act different and just seem older. There is an element of a rite of passage when someone moves closer to the adult world. Based on our cultural mores, sex falls into this category, despite the normative aspect of it for teens. As a midwife, I have seen this happen to girls and it has always struck me as fascinating. One very experienced midwife colleague of mine believes that girls are calmer after having consensual sex for the first time. This colleague has been a midwife longer than I have and puts it this way: "Girls have anxiety about their bodies—form and function—that's alleviated once they have sex. I think it's the power of connection. It's an intensely communicative, social event that is deeply soothing at a time when they are not able and wanting to connect with their parents and they're lonely for contact. If sex was truly consensual, it's likely to have been pleasant and satisfying and this becomes apparent."

I agree with my colleague and consider the rite-of-passage aspects of sexual debuts something girls revere, even if the circumstances or the partner are less than perfect or ideal. There is something inexplicably important and meaningful about everyone's first time, especially when it includes longing and emotional attachment. Think back on this experience for yourself. Chances are it holds significance for you.

The key here is whether or not the sex was really consensual. Girls who have willingly acted on their sexual desires have a changed look and feel about them. Their faces look older and more mature and their stature seems more like a woman's than a teen's. Truth be told, having sex when you're a teenage girl, finding pleasure in it, and planning on having it again is a life-changing event. You become someone you weren't before you made such a decision.

The more willing you are to hear what your daughter has to say about her friends' sexual relationships and possibly her own, the more you'll be able to assess whether or not her peers were in the least bit influential or not. Give her the benefit of the doubt and your undivided attention. Let her say what's on her mind as opposed to dominating the conversation with what's on yours.

QUESTIONS TO ASK YOURSELF

Below are questions to help you clarify your feelings about how your daughter interacts with other people her age, how you feel about her friends and her friendships, and whether or not you are giving your girl the space she needs to succeed in her secret culture of cool.

- Who does my daughter consider to be her closest friends?

- What sorts of things does my daughter do with her friends?

- Do the kids my daughter considers her friends behave in civilized and polite ways or is their behavior disrespectful of others?

- Do I know any of her friends' families? If not, why?

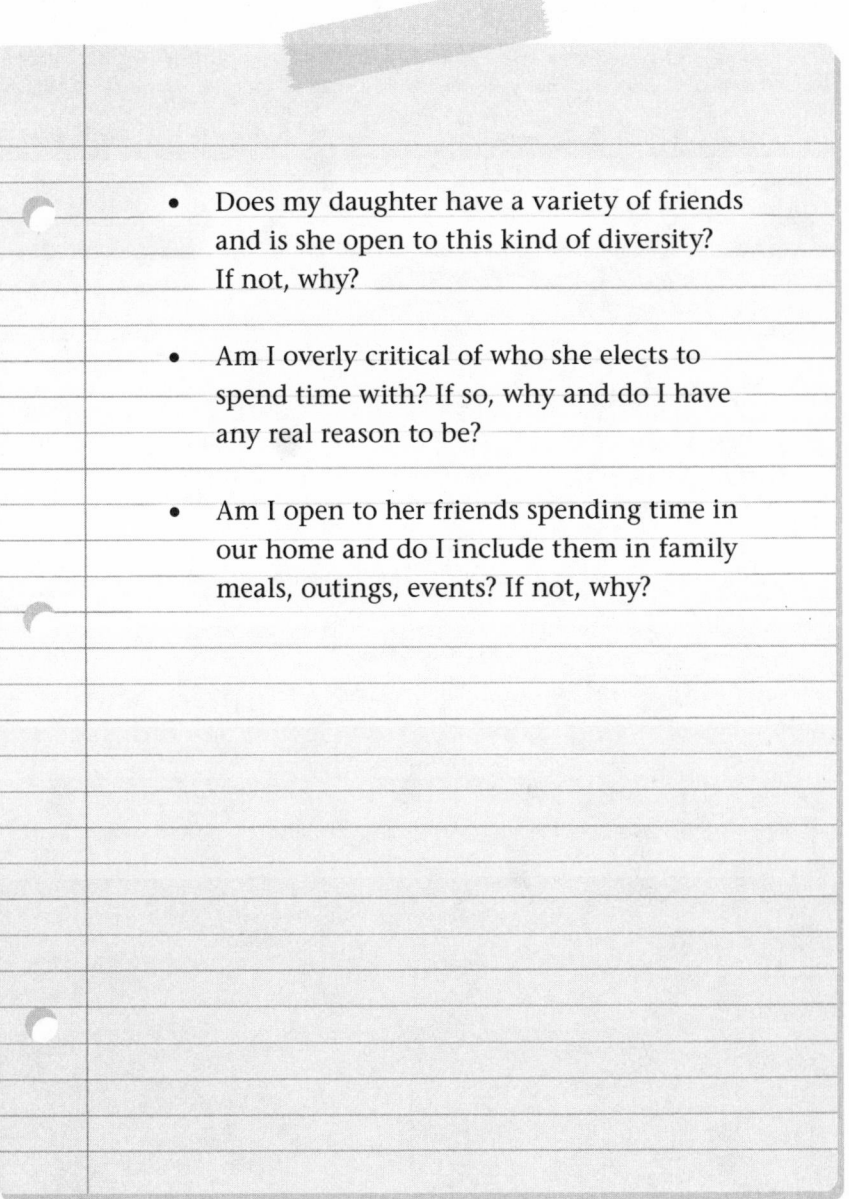

- Does my daughter have a variety of friends and is she open to this kind of diversity? If not, why?

- Am I overly critical of who she elects to spend time with? If so, why and do I have any real reason to be?

- Am I open to her friends spending time in our home and do I include them in family meals, outings, events? If not, why?

CHAPTER 6

THE HIDDEN COSTS OF JUST SAYING NO

"The central agent of eroticism is the human imagination, but for many people the project of sexual self-discovery is hampered by parental messages that induce fear, guilt, and mistrust."

— Esther Perel, *Mating in Captivity*

Parents want the safest passage through adolescence possible for their daughters. I don't know of any parent that hasn't spent plenty of time praying that their kid won't go too far with their rebellious behavior, especially when it comes to school performance, drugs, alcohol, cigarettes, and of course sex. Most of us are willing to accept a combination of A's, B's, and an occasional C and will tolerate brief and limited experimentation with booze, pot, and cigarettes. But when it comes to sexual activity, this seems to fall into a separate category for many parents of girls and they have far less tolerance for experimentation. Because of people's terror, especially of unintended pregnancy, there is a drive to encourage teen girls to avoid sex altogether, no matter what circumstance or conditions they're having it under. This is where the "just say no" abstinence-based fervor has its genesis. People's fear of pregnancy is so intense that they focus on the reproductive hazards of sex exclusively when they talk about sex to their daughters. There is absolutely no mention of the pleasures of sex for fear of encouragement to stray in that direction.

As the parent of a teen girl, especially one who is as bold and fearless as mine, I can identify with this fear and the angst it incites. When I asked my daughter one evening what time she expected that she'd be home and she told me, "Don't you worry, it'll be way past your bedtime," I thought, *Oh no, what is she planning now that this is her answer?* When she was preparing to go out, I was already in my flannel pajamas, tucked into bed with a great magazine—at 9:00 P.M. Before she left, I went into my litany of instructions and parting wisdoms, the same way I did every time she went out and then I settled in and hoped for the best. Eventually I couldn't help but fall into a half-sleep, but I continued to listen with one ear until I heard her come in the door before I could completely surrender to real sleep for the rest of the night.

I have no idea what she was out doing, and by that time in her life (senior year in high school) that was not uncommon. As I have mentioned, it's not as though our community had received the Disney award for good clean fun and I was aware that my daughter socialized with at least some of the offenders who had avoided getting busted. At that point, I had no real choice but to rely on the parenting and examples of conduct I had given her since the day she was born and assume she would refer to whatever fragments of those commandments of good living rose to her consciousness at just the right moments.

Whether or not my daughter had sex while she was out, though, was not something I worried about or fretted over. Probably because of my experience as a midwife and sexuality counselor, I took a completely different approach to sex than most parents did and worried far less about that than drug and alcohol use. I knew if I played my cards right, I could do plenty to help Thalia avoid a sexual crisis. Our public health statistics on teen pregnancy rates and the rising incidence of STIs in teens across socioeconomic lines confirm what I know from my clinical practice: our teenage daughters are engaged in sex more often than not. Most important, though, what these statistics reflect is that teen girls are involved in partnered sex without adequate sex education, contraception, and preventative measures for STIs. This was information I knew I could give her and had no hesitation whatsoever.

Because of my inside view of normal teen behavior and my knowledge of the risks of being uninformed, I decided to start talking about sex early on in my daughter's life and normalize the discussions as much as possible. I openly and seriously discussed the risk of an unintended pregnancy as a possibility, included information about both abortion and teen motherhood as choices under such circumstances, and certainly emphasized that not getting into the situation in the first place was optimal. But I never overemphasized the reproductive facts or hazards of sex as greater than the innate pleasures it held. My information about unintended pregnancies always included information about the methods available to prevent them and that some methods were more effective than others.

Before my daughter was a young teen, she knew that abstinence and same sex relationships were the only things that were 100 percent effective contraceptives. But she also knew about other choices that were available whose efficacy was 98–99 percent when used correctly. Our conversations about sex as a family and as mother and daughter started early in life and referred to an unplanned pregnancy as exactly what it was—a possible outcome under conditions of unprotected and uninformed sex or possibly as the result of a contraceptive method failure.

I also deliberately lived a life I hoped my daughter would choose: monogamous in a loving relationship, focused on the pursuit of life's joys, and openly conversant about sex, sexual desires, sexual health, and healthy sexual behaviors. This included mentioning my own satisfaction with sex and its importance in my life. It was a policy in our household that the adults were not available on weekends and days off until after 9:00 A.M. and that kids were not allowed to knock on our closed door unless the house was on fire or they were bleeding to death. When they asked why, we answered them honestly: "Because we're probably having sex and you'll ruin it and you're definitely not invited." With all this in mind, I also eventually allowed what many parents consider the unthinkable: I let my daughter's steady boyfriend sleep in her room with her, overnight, in our home. My daughter had her first serious long-term relationship when she was 16. She and her boyfriend were a year apart in school and almost two years apart in age, he being older. This is a completely appropriate age difference in any teen couple, heterosexual, lesbian, or gay.

Oliver was a lovely and loveable person and I quickly became fond of him, welcoming him into our home and including him in family meals whenever possible. My daughter knew my general feelings about sex so she had no hesitation about asking me, not long after they started dating, if Oliver could spend the night at our house.

At first, I wasn't sure about my answer. In my mind, I tussled with the consequences of saying yes or no. Was this a good idea? What message would I be conveying if I permitted this? Was this safe? Why did I not automatically say something like other parents did, like "Not in my house you're not," or "If you're going to do that, I better not find out about it!" This was one of those questions I couldn't give an immediate answer to. I told my daughter I would get back to her as soon as possible and that I needed time to ponder.

The more pondering I did, the more I felt that saying no was simply unwarranted and I honestly couldn't come up with substantiation for it. When I imagined actually saying no, it felt wrong, kind of cruel, and intuitively I felt it was shortsighted, although I couldn't completely explain why. I also have a personal belief that when my gut tells me something that my head can't completely rationalize or explain in words, I need to follow my gut. It's often onto something well before my brain is.

When I saw my daughter with her boyfriend, she was often radiant and her smile spoke volumes about her state of mind. They laughed much of the time and clearly enjoyed each other's company and attention. My daughter's grades weren't suffering; she had become a member of a new and more diverse peer group of funny, smart, normal teens; and in short she was happy. A happy teenager is a lovely thing to behold and an incredible relief to a mother whose professional life has shown her the dark side of adolescence much too often. My daughter's disposition was evidence of her sound mental health. Imposing restrictions and limits on her happiness didn't make sense and this included her sexual happiness. And to what end? After I seriously thought about it, I decided to say yes and told my daughter it was okay with me. That was that. But explaining this to his parents was another story.

The calls from his mother started coming right from the beginning. She was irate and simply couldn't come to terms with my decision, insisting that I send him out the door packing. Although I truly liked her, the sound of her voice when she had "that tone" was so personally activating I could barely stand it. Without fail, if she called looking for him and started speaking in that certain way, I ended up feeling like a misbehaving teen myself and was catapulted into a state of anxiety driven by a voice in my head that kept repeating: "Please, let me explain, it's not what you think!"

When confronted with her disapproval on the phone, I respectfully assured her that our adolescent lovebirds were safe in my home, at minimal risk for an unplanned pregnancy (I had made sure my daughter had an effective method of birth control and knew how to use it properly), and enjoying each other's company exclusively. No wild parties, orgies, or drinking contests in a group of hell-raisers. They were watching stupid television wrapped around one another like boa constrictors. The only hazard here was that they might not make it out of the house in case of fire due to their extreme and distracting contentment. But, no matter what I said, the reality of my harboring these fugitives of teen love and lust was more than she could digest.

This mother's sentiment was not unfamiliar to me. After all, I have encountered this on a regular basis in my midwifery practice for over 20 years. Mothers of sexually active teens appear in my office on a regular basis, beside themselves over their daughters' decision to have sex. I should know how to handle this, right? But in those cases, mothers leave my office after a relatively short visit and usually concede to my opinion as the expert. They're not calling me on the phone at home and including my own daughter in their complaints about kids having sex.

For my daughter's sake and because of my commitment to my beliefs, and empathy for this woman's distress, I felt an obligation to do everything I could to turn down the heat and reduce her upset. In addition, as a parent who did not permit alcohol and drug use in my home, I had experienced feeling the same sort of distress when I came up against parents whose house rules about substance use were radically different from mine. Parents who allowed my daughter and their own kids to smoke pot and drink alcohol in their homes were as upsetting to me as I was to Oliver's mother. In fact, there was one household where parents were apparently providing alcoholic beverages on designated party nights and they weren't what anyone would consider fringe or freaky people. They had very different values than I did. Eventually, the mutually agreed upon compromise was that those parents met me halfway in our dispute: they agreed to make the partiers spend the night and make sure their parents knew where they were, thus eliminating the risks of driving while under the influence. To me this was intelligent, cooperative, compromising among parents of varying opinions with the same interest in keeping kids safe. In the spirit of reconciliation, I was determined to find an equal compromise and to communicate successfully and peacefully with Oliver's mother.

I told her that I respected her opinion, but didn't share it. I also felt that it wasn't my role to be her spokesperson. The discussion needed to change arenas and participants and should involve her husband and Oliver—I was officially out. I ended with this comment: the problem we were wrangling with was not about safety. It was about values. We had different values and didn't seem to be able to come to any agreeable conclusion about how to bridge the gap between opinions. As well-intentioned parents we should have been able to amiably end the strife by simply agreeing to disagree. But this wasn't the case. I also sensed that this mother was having a hard time letting her youngest child make some decisions on his own and coming to terms with her real inability to control his behavior.

During the remainder of his romance with my daughter, Oliver's relationship with his mother deteriorated. It had become abundantly clear that her fury about values had backfired and the communication and trust between she and her son had broken down. His defiance became his crusade and the relationship with his parents suffered. His family became the enemy. Any guidance, mentoring, or advice they could have provided was lost in the battle over the literal embodiment and expression of his love and desire.

Eventually, as Oliver neared graduation and was soon to be headed on his way out the door, things calmed down. In preparation for graduation and leaving the nest, perhaps it became clear to his mother that Oliver was soon to be completely out of her purview and she would have no say or idea of what he would be doing.

One would think that after all this that the actual costs of saying no would have been completely clear to me. But, it wasn't until two years later that I actually heard myself articulate the real rationale behind my decision to let Oliver spend the night.

I often speak in salon forums—groups of 15–40 women, between the ages of 35 and 45, who gather at the home of a comrade in parenting, seeking counsel about raising their "impossible" teenage daughters. They come to share their ideas and frustrations with other women trying to survive their daughters' adolescence and who are also feeling like failures in the process.

There is always someone in these audiences who finds my liberal attitudes about teen girls and sex so enraging they can barely stay in their seat. Regardless of where I am or the etiquette of the moment, these women will pop up like a jack-in-the-box spewing their disagreement like molten lava. It never fails. No matter how early on I sense their presence and location in the audience, they startle me every time! I've come to expect this and simply consider it part of the territory. Their level of objection is commensurate with how angry they feel at what I've just said and the confidence with which I've said it. Once I catch my breath and my heart goes back to its normal rhythm, I am usually able to disarm them with humor and my years of expertise. But there's an exception to every rule.

One evening when I was recounting having sanctioned my daughter's sleeping arrangements with her boyfriend, a woman in the audience who had been making me nervous from the beginning of the night finally blew out of her seat like Old Faithful. It was clear she simply couldn't contain her anger for one more second and proceeded to launch into a fierce rebuttal and criticism of me and my parenting. With sparks shooting from her eyeballs, she concluded her diatribe with a kind of summative question: "Don't you think your daughter would have had a different experience of this if you had made her wait until she was 22 instead of 16?" Frankly, at first I didn't understand the question, but, surprisingly, this worked to my advantage.

By this time, my limbic brain and amygdala were so activated with a sense of threat I was having physical symptoms. My back was covered with sweat, my mouth was as dry as the Sahara, and I was having shortness of breath. Stalling for time, I took a sip of water, deliberately slowed down my breathing and silently begged my forebrain to come to my rescue. Knowing my mind as I do, I knew I must have a decent and meaningful response to this. But where was it in my data bank?! Suddenly, as if I had consulted the Magic Eight Ball, I started to channel a calm, confident, and completely new voice. I responded with this answer: "Yes, of course she would have had a different experience if I had made her wait. She'll be a different person when she's 22 than when she was 16. But being different when you're older doesn't have anything to do with being allowed to enjoy your body and sexuality sooner, rather than later, especially given that she was doing so safely and with minimal risk."

A hush spread across the room and everyone was quiet, including my argumentative opponent. All eyes were upon me. I found out later that my response had struck a chord with many people in the audience. As for me, I experienced clarity and coalescence about my decision two years prior that was different than it had ever been before. It was a seminal moment. Two years later, I realized that had I said no to my daughter's request, I would have denied her an experience that was rightfully hers, repressed her sense of fearless enjoyment in her sexual expression, and jeopardized my open communication with her. I also would have been a complete hypocrite. And if there's anything teenagers cannot tolerate and will ferret out it is hypocrisy.

When sexual energy knocks loudly at the door of your daughter's body and soul, answer it with her and welcome this relative stranger in with your approval. In fact, introduce them to one another. Those of us who would rather our girls ignore the knocking until they're married or we're dead fail to realize the terrific opportunity this provides us as parents to positively influence our daughters' sexual behavior and reduce risk taking in general. It will also grant parents insight and access to a new view of your daughter at a fantastic time in her development as a human being. Think of it. Parents who say no to sex unequivocally—as Oliver's mother had—often end up with kids who drift from them and don't let them get near any part of their heart at a time when it's getting bigger and deeper. When you take your daughter's longings seriously and don't automatically veto them, you're likely to stay closer to her through her adolescence than you would otherwise.

Remembering that the forbidden fruit is always the sweetest and most tempting is also helpful. This can relate to anything: Halloween candy, television viewing, Internet use, and sex. Whatever is forbidden will undoubt-edly be the very thing most longed for and sought after. Complicating matters further is the fact that parents who have the belief that having sex is a completely bad idea are working against the forces of nature that are always stronger than we are.

Sexual illiteracy, an unwillingness to communicate about anything, resentment toward you because you invalidate her feelings of love and longing for some-one—these are the side effects of a girl who can't openly communicate with her mother. Your daughter has little choice but to keep secrets from you about the person she is becoming. As far as she's concerned, you don't really want to know about what she's experiencing anyway.

As a midwife who is regularly in the position of listen-ing to girls who feel this way, I recommend that mothers do everything they can to prevent this from happening. The estrangement that results when this is the status quo between mothers and daughters has ill effects that can linger well into adulthood when independent decision making becomes so important and long-term relational bonds are forged.

Sometimes the tactics mothers use to dissuade their girls from becoming sexually active include some degree of shame in an attempt to shape and influence their behavior. I didn't fully realize or understand the extent of this until I had been in practice as a sexuality coun-selor for several years. After listening to many women's descriptions of problems they were having enjoying sex, I started to make the connection between what my teen patients experienced and the sexual and relational prob-lems of the adult women I cared for. Elements of sexual mastery— limited risk taking, a strong self and body image, protective intuition, physical health, knowledge of human anatomy, familiarity and comfort with what pleases us sexually, and the feeling that sexual satisfaction is a basic human right—grow best under the conditions present in adolescence. The plasticity of the human brain is greatest up until the age of 20.[1] This is when human psychology and biochemistry combine and make the most fertile conditions for these roots to take hold. When this is interrupted, stunted, or suppressed, girls struggle to make up for the lost opportunity later in life, and this is never easy.

My client Jane is representative of many women I work with who have told me that they believe their feelings about sex and their sexual identity are inextricably linked to events that occurred in their adolescence and experiences and interactions they had with their mothers. In Jane's case, this was especially true and it took years for her to untangle this terrible snarl.

It was an early spring day in March, she was 14, and Jane was walking, wearing pants, a white turtleneck, and a coat. She described feeling happy and carefree from the change in season and because of the increased temperature, she was walking with her coat unbuttoned. She then saw her family driving toward her smiled at the surprise of it and happy to see them so unexpectedly. Then she noticed a look of disdain on her mother's face and a terrible sense of confusion and dread came over her. She couldn't imagine why her mother looked this way.

When she arrived home, her mother slapped her across the face and asked her what she thought she was doing walking with her "chest displayed" and told her:

"You looked like a whore." What had started out as a happy, innocent experience at 14 became one of terrible confusion and long-lasting pain. Jane explains: "I still remember this so clearly. I can feel it. The background fades and the camera comes in close on the event in my mind."

This particular experience is an extreme example of what mothers are capable of. But I have worked with so many women who have been called slut, whore, and tramp by their mothers at various points during their adolescence and although physical abuse may not have been involved, the pain of their verbal cruelty has been equally hurtful and long-lasting. Sadly, these kinds of epithets are not uncommon and they leave lasting negative memories and impressions.

Some parent advocates and sympathizers have told me that these comments and events are simply misunderstandings on the part of daughters whose mothers were acting out of goodness and in the best interests of their daughter's safety. As a woman, mother, and midwife, I don't buy it!

Many women come to see me for sexuality counseling in middle age. Once their children don't need their attention every minute, they begin the process of life assessment that normally occurs in our 40s and 50s. The decade between 45 and 55 is especially ripe for review. Women realize they're facing the last half of their lives and it's not uncommon for them to evaluate their overall feelings of satisfaction. For some women this includes their satisfaction with sex—as individuals and in relationship to a partner, if they have one.

In either case—single or coupled—what many women describe is a sense of estrangement or distance from their sexual identity. They'll openly admit to me that this has existed for years but for varied reasons, they did nothing to change it. Now that they're facing the last half of their lives, the thought of never having joyful, exuberant, and deeply satisfying sex is simply untenable. The courage of middle age empowers them to seek, and sometimes demand, the kind of sexual experiences they truly want: lusty, orgasmic, intense, and full of desire. It's the kind of sex that we ideally become well acquainted with and form a deep bond to in adolescence when the biological support makes it easiest to do so. Yet few of us are given this opportunity.

Sometimes they have experienced this with lovers in the past. Or they'll tell me about current relationships with paramours where this is alive and well. In these cases, I am talking with women who I refer to as having married the family dog: a partner that's handsome, loyal, devoted, won't stray, great with kids, and friendly to everyone. These women appreciate these features but they're not sexy to them and they don't feel any more attracted to these men as sex partners than they do the family's golden retriever. They married them because their parents—and everyone else—approved, not because the sexual chemistry was there from the beginning, and loved their partner because this was a feature of their relationship they wanted to sustain. This is a particularly sad but common outcome in many marriages and the complexities that it presents at middle age are especially vexing and burdensome.

There's also another group of women who come for counseling. These are women who don't feel sexually confident, don't fully understand how their bodies work or the names of all parts of their genitalia, and may have long-standing difficulty achieving orgasm. Women who have never had an orgasm or are having difficulty having one are often unfamiliar with the value and benefits of self-pleasuring and frequently don't know what they need to know about their genitalia to maximize their likelihood of being orgasmic, either alone or with a partner. More often than not, this results from having been discovered while masturbating and subsequently shamed and embarrassed by the person who found them—usually their mother.

Unlike boys and men who often walk around fondling their genitals—nearly absentmindedly—with no negative commentary or consequence, girls who engage in similar behaviors are frequently told their hands are dirty, or it's not ladylike. Rarely do parents use this as an opportunity to tell girls the names of their genitals, including the clitoris. Further, the vulva, along with its contents, is rarely specifically named. It is the vagina that reigns supreme in our vernacular to describe a girl's genitalia. The organ that is the most sensitive and enervated and whose sole purpose is to provide pleasure—the clitoris—goes unidentified, unmentioned, and unnamed.

The idea that masturbation is a normal activity for girls and women couldn't be farther from their consciousness or general knowledge about what is normal for sexually desirous girls and women.

Women struggling with these problems frequently tell me they believe these feelings erupted secondary to ways their sexuality was addressed—or not—when it came into the foreground in adolescence. Many report having lived in families where the silence about sex was so deafening and persistent that the risks of breaking it felt earth-shattering. No one discussed the topic and it was made clear, on an energetic level, that this simply wasn't a sanctioned topic of conversation.

I'll never forget the time my mother called me a tramp and slut because she found out I had had sex with my boyfriend—I was 17. She also was convinced I was pregnant. I tried to tell her over and over again that I was taking birth control pills but she was so irate this didn't matter to her. Somehow, it felt like I had committed the worst crime, given what she was saying. I felt so bruised from this and she's never apologized. It was one of the most embarrassing and upsetting experiences of my life and I'm not sure I've ever really forgiven her for it. I feel like that experience might have put a permanent wet blanket on my love life. I never have really enjoyed sex. I have never been able to have an orgasm. I don't masturbate—that seems weird and dirty to me. I'd rather do just about anything than have sex.

— Chantal, 44

When I move between appointments with teen girls who need to conceal their sexual activity from their mothers to my consult room where I talk with adult women who have come asking for help to increase their sexual satisfaction, the connection is evident. There is a commonality of experience between these patients even though they may be more than a generation apart. What they're both likely to describe having are mothers who were pedantic about their teachings regarding the dangers and problems inherent in sex. Their tactics are commonly shaming and personally degrading and the humiliation they rely on to dissuade their girls from sexual activity can be quite persistent. They never mention anything about sex being pleasant or joyful.

I was very pretty as a teenager and I had lots of boys interested in me. My mother made it perfectly clear to me that only cheap and fast girls had sex and I wasn't one of those girls. She would tell me that all boys wanted when they were my age was sex. She said they would say they loved me, get what they wanted and then dump you. And if I got pregnant, I'd never see the boy again. It gave me a terrible feeling about my own interest in my boyfriend and definitely made me question his interest in me, and I've been suspicious of men's interest in me ever since. I guess it's no surprise that I've never found a partner that I feel I can trust.

— Fiona, 42

Although our daughters' rebellious behavior and turned-off expressions can easily lead us to believe that they're ignoring everything we say and do when it comes to sex, this is clearly not the case. Mothers often interpret their daughters' having sex against parental mandate as synonymous with disregarding of how they've been instructed to behave. Based on my experience with teens and adults, this is not the case. If it were, then teenagers—with all their rebellious energy and drive—would be more openly defiant about their activity and adult women wouldn't continue to suffer from the residual effects of their mothers' negative comments and actions years prior.

Teenage girls know we must know something more than they do about the subject, if for no other reason than we've been alive longer than they have. I'm not suggesting that mothers share all their sexual secrets, exploits, and proclivities with their daughters. But I am suggesting that giving your daughter the advantage of some of your experiences and knowledge will work to her benefit, not her detriment.

Sexually content and satisfied women who come to me to help them spice things up with their sex lives almost always tell me they had mothers who talked about sex as one of life's sweetest and most pleasing experiences. They also describe how their mothers often displayed a sense of comfort with their bodies, expressed their sexuality in visible ways around their daughters, were complimentary of their daughters' maturing figures (no matter what they looked like), and were easily able to talk about sex as a great part of life. Even when these mothers had strong feelings about girls maintaining abstinence until a certain age or even until marriage, they made it clear that sex was an essential ingredient of a successful, long-term relationship and sustained happiness in love.

They also instilled a sense in their daughter that there were many ways to experience feeling and being sexy that aren't dependent on being in a sexual relationship. Clothing choices, sensual activities like dancing and enjoying fantasies, choosing different music for different moods, massages, and masturbating are all means by which to enjoy ones sexual energy that don't depend on being involved with someone. This is a radically different approach from the norm.

My mother's behavior was really interesting, now that I look back on it. She certainly had a kind of reserve that was typical for the time. But, there was no question that she and my father were having sex—and often! They adored each other and my sisters and I saw evidence of this all the time. She would sit on his lap, he would put his arms around her and kiss her when she was washing dishes—things like that. And she would say things to us like: "Girls, what your father and I do when we're alone is one of the things that makes our marriage so great. I hope you're as lucky as we are when you get married." She never came out and said anything like: "Dad and I have great sex." But we all knew that's what she meant and that they really were crazy about each other—they still carry on and they're both in their mid-70s.

I distinctly remember my mother telling me once, I must have been about three or four, that touching my "private spot" was okay and that she knew it felt good to me and that it feels good to everyone. She added that I needed to do this in private, but I didn't feel shamed by her or embarrassed. Later in life, I was looking for something in her bedside drawer and I found a vibrator. I was about 40 and I was mortified! She came into the room and I said to her: "So Mom, what's with this?" She told me that even though she didn't have a partner anymore (my father had died) that she enjoyed herself all on her own sometimes and that this was normal. She then asked me if I wanted her to get one for me!

— Beth, 58

There is no statute of limitations on experiencing pleasure in our bodies and sexual pleasure is no exception. For some of us the nature, frequency, interest, and types of sexual activities we engage in will change as we age. Ideally, the combination of skin and soul that is our greatest sexual organ is steadfast throughout life and begins to take hold and be shaped in our teens. We would serve our daughters best if we helped them begin the process of refining this in adolescence. If we chose to control our fears about sex and see it as less about reproduction and more about pleasure we could lay a completely different foundation upon which to build our own sex education curricula, as well as a better foundation for our daughter's future sexual health than we ourselves had.

Undoubtedly many of you are thinking that sexual passion and pleasure are the sole province of the young and that we shouldn't expect to match those sorts of feelings in middle age or beyond. Many of us also believe that in long-term marriages passion always wanes and we shouldn't have the unrealistic expectation that we will stay lustful. This is not the case for everyone. There are long-term couples of all ages who are still having great sex after 30 years of marriage or more. Women who feel this way tell me that they've always loved sex, many from the time they were teens. They tell me that they have made a point of keeping the heat of sexual passion and pleasure a priority and actively work on cultivating the essence of their sexual energy. They come to me to ask for assistance on how to become more exploratory, or to find out about sex toys they've never seen before, or to ask about new things to do that perhaps they just haven't thought of yet. These visits are with women who display a degree of sexual sophistication that has developed as a result of devotion to their sexual pleasure. And they almost always have been raised by mothers who had very positive attitudes about sex, not negative ones. Mothers who are open about the pleasures and joys of sexual expression have insight into the costs of saying no when it comes to their daughter's long-term sexual happiness. They also tend to be women who enjoy sex themselves and they want their daughters to feel this way too.

As mothers, it falls to us to foster a friendly and positive relationship between our daughters and their bodies, which includes teaching our daughters to listen to their impulses, to satisfy their desires, and to explore what gives them pleasure, so that they can develop the positive body confidence and body friendly perspective that they will need to live long, happy and fulfilling adult lives.

QUESTIONS TO ASK YOURSELF

Although many of us would just as soon forget this time in our lives, few of us would deny that our teen years profoundly influenced who we became as adults. Before going on, consider the following questions and relate them to both your experience and your daughters.

- Are there things I wish I had said yes to but didn't because I was afraid of what my mother would think, say, or do to me?

- What relationships have I said yes to out of my need to feel like I was pleasing my parents first?

- Do I feel like I struggle with sex because of things my mother said to me about my body, behavior, or my sexual interest? If so, what are they?

- Do I repeat some of the things my mother said to me about sex to my daughter and if so, do I think this is a good idea?

- Was I sexually promiscuous and if so, do I know why?

- Does saying yes to sex always mean you're "easy" or that you aren't discriminating if you're a teen girl?

- Do I feel like I am partnered in a long-term relationship with someone who sexually satisfies me, or did I marry for other reasons?

- Under what circumstances is it okay with me if my daughter says yes to sex?

CHAPTER 7

THE FOUNDATION OF A HEALTHY SEXUALITY

"If sex and creativity are often seen by dictators
as subversive activities, it's because they lead to the knowledge
that you own your own body (and with it your voice) and that's
the most revolutionary insight of all."

— Erica Jong

The desire for companionship, communion, and connection—emotional and physical—is powerful in human beings, and we seek it at every stage of development. Barring any major disruptions in our rearing and in the absence of serious psychiatric disorders, we all seek feelings of being bonded and attached to other people. We flourish when we have these vital connections in our lives, and we wither when we do not.

In the beginning of life, our need for connection is met by loving family members and, most important, mothers. As we age and develop our personalities and a greater sense of individuality emerges, we transfer this need, in all its forms, to other, non-parental relationships.

As teen girls first seek the touch of another, particularly intimate touch, they begin to develop mastery over their minds, bodies, self, and sexual identity. It helps them discover their likes and dislikes, aids them in establishing the foundation of healthy sexuality, and can ultimately make a difference between leading a sexually fulfilling life or not. Teenage girls must be given the opportunity to fully develop all aspects of themselves. As grown women, our daughters must have good mental health and a strong sense of self for a joyful and happy life; if absent, women can suffer extraordinarily when it comes to sex.

Although I am not trained as a psychotherapist or mental health practitioner, my assessment skills of a patient's mental health have developed out of necessity. Caring for teens and women for over 20 years has led me to create a system of evaluation that I implement every time I work with someone, regardless of their age. This evaluation focuses on six critical markers of emotional well-being, each intricately connected to how a woman experiences sexual interest, satisfaction, and proficiency. These markers are self-esteem; health-seeking behaviors, such as specific diet and exercise practices; optimism; creativity; compassion for self and others; and sense of humor. My patients have given me a fantastic opportunity to witness and study how the combination of these strengths can help them achieve satisfying sexual experiences. When all these virtues are present, substantial, and actively deployed, people are powerful and able to move through experiences, both good and bad, with a sturdiness of spirit that offers resilience and protection against life's tribulations.

Recently a teen came to see me who taught me so much about the connection between women, sex, power, and confidence. Her story, though painful, is inspiring. Her sense of self remained so intact that it's impossible not to feel motivated and uplifted in spite of the terrible situation that brought her to me in the first place.

Claire came in, accompanied by her mother, in an acute state of illness. She had never had a sexual experience until she was the victim of rape. After her assault, she became horribly sick with a primary outbreak of genital herpes. By the time I saw her, she hadn't eaten or been able to urinate in two days. She had a fever and was in terrible pain due to multiple lesions on her genitals. At 18, Claire was the same age as my daughter and this made caring for her very personal to me.

My first order of business was to prescribe medication to treat her pain and help her empty her bladder. I also prescribed antiviral medication to shorten the course of this first outbreak. I knew she would need plenty of emotional support, as did her mother, given the circumstances. With my medical care complete, I ended my visit by telling her that what had happened was not her fault and that although I was sure it didn't seem this way to her now, she would recover. I also asked her to come back to see me in a week or so. We could talk more when she was feeling better.

I didn't see Claire for a couple more months and when she did return, I barely recognized her. She was preparing to go off to college, had cut her hair and looked much older and somehow wiser. I couldn't quite figure it out. She was completely recovered physically, and when I asked how she was feeling emotionally, she said: "I am doing pretty well. I confronted the man who raped me and told him what he had done to me and how it made me feel. Even though I don't plan on pressing charges, it was so good to do what I did, and I am sure it has helped."

Facing and confronting a rapist is one of the most difficult things any woman can do and this certainly must
have been true for Claire. Yet she had tremendous composure and great support from a loving mother who cared
for her deeply. Claire told me her mother had always been
this way and that she had always felt close to her.

I did my exam, and when I finished, I asked Claire
how she felt about the possibility of having sex with
someone given that she was likely to meet people at
college. She looked at me and smiled and, in the most
compassionate way, made it clear that she wasn't ready for
this—yet. She knew she would be someday, but it was too
soon to think about now. She needed more time to heal
and promised to come back to see me when she needed
my help. She felt better about herself, was taking care of
her health, and was about to start a big creative endeavor
by going to college. Not to mention that I could see her
humor coming back to life. I knew that Claire would be
fine and that her mother had played a major role in her
recovery and wellness.

Claire had the essential ingredients of self-esteem
and confidence and the other markers of emotional well-
being. She was a great gift to me as a midwife and her
mother reminded me of the tremendous value of kind
and attentive mothering. She inspired me in my work
and as a mother myself.

The development and maturation of a healthy sexual
foundation is best fostered during adolescence, when our
daughters' sexuality is emerging and highly sensitive
to outside influences, especially those of the parents. A
mother's example and focus while parenting go a long

way in building self-esteem and inspiring strong health-seeking behaviors, optimism, creativity, compassion, and humor.

When we notice that our girls are starting to flirt and express interest in a sexual partner, it's critically important for us to stay clear-headed and kind. Many of us fear that if we discuss our daughters' emerging sexuality, it will seem as if we are opening the door to reckless behavior. In my experience as a midwife, sexual promiscuity is not the norm. Girls who are promiscuous are often teens who lack maternal attention, guidance, and support. It's also frequently indicative of a history of sexual abuse. [1]

Being a sexually active teen is not the same as being a sexually promiscuous teen. The impact of promiscuity on peer relationships and self-esteem can be devastating. I truly don't believe that girls choose sexual promiscuity because they feel it's a good idea. If a girl is promiscuous and perceived as being casual about who she has sex with, or is known to have multiple partners, her peers are the ones most likely to label her a slut. Sexually promiscuous girls rarely have high self-esteem, and their other markers of emotional well-being are weak at best. It simply isn't an indicator of healthy sexual development.

On the other hand, if your daughter identifies herself as a paragon of virtue based on her commitment to abstinence and wouldn't even consider having a sweetheart, her behavior is out of the norm too. For parents, this may come as a relief, but her peers are going to think she is strange. Once again, the cost of taking an extreme and abnormal stance will appear in social connections with peers. The abstinence mongers in your local high school don't necessarily feel greater confidence or self-worth than the high school whore. Neither girl is particularly confident about who she is.

Belonging to a group that defines itself—in the way they dress, their common interests, taste in music, and sexual experience—gives teen girls credible identification and acceptance in the greater social order. And working to be part of this group will often drive your daughter away from what you would consider the norm. Adolescents conduct experiments in all aspects of living, including drugs, alcohol, and sexuality. Sometimes you may think that these explorations are going too far, but when dealing with teens, your continuum for normal experimentation needs to be elasticized to some extent. This is the time when our daughters are growing and stretching their limbs. These are signs of health and the formation of emotional markers of well-being. What they need through the process are brief, yet repetitive reminders of health and safety, in combination with visible evidence of healthy living from parents as the backdrop on which to compare their behaviors.

As a mother, I did everything in my power to solidify my daughter's markers of emotional well-being. And now her loves and talents reflect that she has developed into a confident older teen who is true to herself and her sexuality. She knows who she is and what she needs without being subject to the whims of those around her.

On a recent visit home from college (she is a freshman), laundry in tow and with big plans for baking and cooking projects, my daughter began a spontaneous conversation with me that demanded my full attention. It was all about drugs and sex among her college peers and former high school classmates. My job was to sit and listen attentively and speak only when spoken to directly. Doing so would give me the greatest amount of information possible and just the fact that she started talking to me about this stuff meant she had something she wanted me to know—and that she trusted me.

What I heard about the scene in general was not surprising, but it was disturbing. There's a lot of drinking and drug use on the campus of her state university and evidently our small town's Main Street drug mall has worsened, with new entertainment drugs available at relatively low cost. Thalia was lamenting the excess usage of these drugs by many of her friends. In her semi-monologue, she would ask rhetorically, "What's the *draw*?" It was genuinely confounding to her that the myriad extracurricular activities she'd discovered on campus could be less interesting than getting high. She was upset, disappointed in her friends, and most important, making a clear distinction between herself and them. This was a very good sign.

I watch my daughter move through the world with a sense of self-confidence and joy that makes me feel we both survived the turbulence of adolescence intact. She has a great sense of humor and we definitely spend plenty of time laughing heartily, even when the joke is at my expense. As for her compassion, during the holiday season, she asked if I would be willing to match her contribution for gift certificates for both the janitors in her dorm. She told me: "The kids in my dorm are total pigs, and they trash the bathrooms and vomit and leave it for them to clean up. I know these people hardly make any money, and I would like to give them something to show them that I notice and appreciate their work." I nearly crashed my car while trying to manage the tears in my eyes.

When a teenage girl can find balance in her sexuality and strength in each area of her well-being it gives her a noticeable confidence and sturdiness that has an erotic and sexy charge that attracts those around her. Self-confidence is very sexy stuff.

Think about a woman you know who is not physically attractive in any classical sense, but who is extraordinarily appealing and may even be inexplicably "hot." This is a woman folks look at and think, *What is it about her? She is always surrounded by people, and she always looks happy. Gee, she's got something going there—and despite the fact that she's not all that beautiful, she sure has sex appeal.* With rare exception, this is a woman whose markers of emotional well-being are present and accounted for. Most likely, these seeds of confidence were planted during her adolescence. Confidence can have a profound impact on the sexual health of a teen whose body and soul are evolving into a woman's.

I give a weekly lecture at Canyon Ranch and the focus of the lecture is the relationship between confidence and sex appeal. I tell my audiences that if the markers of emotional well-being never take shape and hold early in life or if they're challenged over a long period of time in adulthood, interest in sex will be affected, possibly for a lifetime. It is this confidence that allows a woman to explore her deepest, most intimate passions and dreams. A severe lack of confidence can not only inhibit a woman sexually but emotionally, as she may begin to doubt her self-worth creatively, academically, or professionally.

Lengthy episodes of strife and low self-esteem create the strongest anti-aphrodisiacs of all. When either of these undermining forces is present, women show up in my office searching for answers as to why sex is the last thing on their minds. Or why sex has never felt good or interested them in the first place. In order to relate to someone on the most naked level, we first need to like ourselves and recognize what we have to offer. Further, feeling good about yourself is something you alone possess, and it can grant you the power to say yes to sex—and really mean it—no matter what age you are.

Elizabeth is a patient of mine who exemplifies what I am talking about. At 42, with a successful career as a lawyer, a loving partner, and three healthy children, she was diagnosed with breast cancer. Because of her age, the type of cancer she had, and concerns about recurrence, Elizabeth and her team of health-care providers decided that a bilateral mastectomy was the wisest treatment. This would eliminate her need for chemotherapy, which she had hoped to avoid. She also decided not to have reconstructive surgery because of the lengthened recovery period and need for repetitive procedures.

Elizabeth came to me less than a year after her surgery, when family life was essentially back to normal. When I asked her how I could help, she told me that she had no interest in sex anymore and this was stressful and sad to her. She had always had a satisfying sexual relationship with her husband but since her diagnosis and surgery, her sexual energy had disappeared. Her husband had reassured her that the absence of her breasts was not affecting his attraction to her, but this didn't matter. She described feeling estranged from her body and her sexual energy.

Throughout our visit, I asked questions about her self-confidence, body image, optimism, health practices, and creative outlets throughout life both before and since her diagnosis. I also listened closely for evidence of compassion toward self and for signs of an intact sense of humor. I needed insight into her internal strengths and resources which I could draw on to help her begin to recover her sexuality.

Fortunately, Elizabeth's body image had always been positive. She had been a swimmer and loved the way it made her feel but had resisted getting back into the pool because of the changes in her figure after the surgery. After a woman has survived a serious illness, reacquainting her with the places where she once felt strong and capable is an excellent place to begin to help her restore her confidence in her body.

I looked for evidence of Elizabeth's compassion toward herself. Given what she had gone through, she certainly needed it. Although things were life-as-usual on the outside, she didn't feel normal on the inside and she felt angry with herself for taking time to recover. She had let go of habits and activities which were strengthening and pleasurable for her that she had built into her life since adolescence. At her core, Elizabeth was a confident person with good self-esteem, but life had thrown her a big curve. She felt vulnerable to her health and unconsciously checked out of her body. As a consequence, she also lost track of her identity as a sexual person and her interest in sex became a memory from the past.

I advised her to schedule time out of every week for swimming and other indulgences—massages, socializing with supportive friends, reading for pleasure, napping, and even for crying spells when she felt so inclined. Such things would bring her pleasure and pleasure feeds on itself once it takes hold.

Our consultation ended on a bright note. Elizabeth was relieved that her disinterest in sex was normal given the extreme stress in her life. She appreciated my reassurance that her sexual energy would resurface on its own once she was feeling better, emotionally and physically. I explained that she had the raw ingredients necessary to reconnect with her sexuality but that her markers of emotional well-being had been eroded by her illness and surgery. What I said to her resonated intuitively. She didn't fully understand what I was telling her but it "felt right" and this was all she needed to encourage her to implement my suggestions.

Working with Elizabeth was relatively easy. My role was to identify her inner resources and confidence and give them back to her. I used them to organize an intervention that I have seen help women recover their sense of self and sexuality. She developed these markers early on in life and was fortunate to have had insightful mothering throughout her childhood that helped establish them. In this case, she simply had lost track of them because of life's unexpected turn.

Elizabeth told me that her mother had always been supportive, set a good example of a healthy lifestyle—including a healthy sexual relationship with Elizabeth's father—and always referred to sex as one of life's greatest pleasures. This was, in part, why she was so saddened by her loss of interest. This made it much easier for me to help her and I was certain she would reclaim her feelings of sexiness and sexual prowess as soon as her self-confidence came back.

Lisa, another patient who came to my private practice, represents the other end of the spectrum, and shares the experience and background of many of the patients I see for counseling. Both she and Elizabeth shared a disinterest in sex, but their reasons couldn't have been more dissimilar. In Lisa's case she had few raw ingredients to work with and it made her quest for sexual satisfaction far more difficult.

Lisa was a pleasant, intelligent and attractive 56-year-old woman who came to see me complaining of difficulty having orgasms, with a partner or when masturbating. She had a history of being involved with both male and female partners over the past 15 years and described herself as a "sexual failure, no matter who I am with." That kind of statement is always a red flag in my office and it wasn't long after she sat down before she was tearful and distraught over all that hadn't happened for her.

I began, as I always do, by asking questions about her life and trying to get information about her sense of self and confidence. Not surprisingly, she didn't think much of herself and her confidence had reached an all-time low when she separated from her last partner six months before. She told me that she simply couldn't find anything about herself that made her feel good. This included her appearance and her body in general.

Lisa was attractive, stylish and appeared healthy. There was nothing about her physically that was unappealing, yet her demeanor reflected a negative self-image. She slumped over in her chair and had difficulty keeping eye contact. Her voice was low and she spoke with hesitancy, as if she questioned the worth of her statements. At this point, I took a giant leap of faith and asked her to tell me about her relationship with her mother and her sexual experiences as a teen. Ah, Pandora's box! The words she used to describe her feelings were halting: "Terrible, horrendous, humiliating."

Lisa's mother had been preoccupied with both her appearance and Lisa's and she described her as critical about "everything." When it came to sex, both her mother and father had made it clear that they absolutely didn't approve of her being sexually active. Furthermore, Lisa's mother often turned to her daughter as a confidante and openly discussed her unsatisfying sexual relationship with Lisa's father. This inappropriate disclosure of complicated information coupled with a sex negative model of parenting had far-reaching, negative effects on Lisa. In this case, the life experience of her mother became a template for her and led her to anticipate the worst from sex.

By the time Lisa came to me, she was so crippled by her history, low self-esteem, and experiences of relational and sexual "failures" that she had become depressed and had lost faith in ever being able to achieve pleasure in herself or in a relationship with an intimate partner.

The best I could do in my capacity as a sexuality counselor was to help her gain insight into why she felt so bad and to connect her experiences as a teen with her experiences as an adult. Many women believe that the two are truly separate—one is in the past, the other is in the present. But this really isn't the case and it's often helpful to revisit the past—even briefly—to better understand the struggles of the present. Our lives begin in childhood within the social structure of our families and all of our ways of being and feeling are influenced by this history.

Lisa agreed that she had become depressed and was willing to see a practitioner who could comprehensively assess her mental health and perhaps recommend an antidepressant for her. She told me about other symptoms that she was having that confirmed my suspicions that she was depressed. These included poor sleep, a loss of interest in things and people, body aches, and extreme irritability. I told her I would continue working with her but that her sexual issues were secondary to her managing her depression and addressing her problem of low self-esteem. As is true with many women, Lisa's markers of emotional well-being had not been strengthened throughout her life but her distress about sex and relationships is what finally drove her to seek help. I understood her sexual dissatisfactions were in her foreground, but they couldn't be resolved until her overall emotional health was improved.

Compare my patient Elizabeth with my patient Lisa. As a mother of a teen, which woman represents the kind of adult woman you hope your daughter will become? There is no question that Lisa will struggle most of all and we can trace this all back to her low self-esteem, limited ability to self-soothe, poor coping skills, and negative body image.

While it may be disconcerting for mothers to face the reality of girls choosing an intimate partner to share their loving feelings, a mother's responsibility is to address this shift in their daughter's attention in the privacy of her own heart, mind, or therapy session. Mothers also need to listen to the voice of their own sexual experiences— past and present—and look at them insightfully, with an eye for comparing the ways in which they are the same and different as those they see their daughter managing. Though you may feel inspired to share all of your past experiences, negative and positive, with your daughter, it is important to keep in mind the impact they may have on her outlook.

If you're parenting a teen girl, do all you can to keep in mind that one day, sooner than you imagine, the daughter you are living with now will be a woman who longs for many of the same things you do—love, sexual satisfaction, peace of mind, and the highest self-regard possible. Your contributions to her feeling powerful in herself will serve her well through life, no matter what age she is.

QUESTIONS TO ASK YOURSELF

Your answers to the questions below will hopefully give you a deeper understanding of your sense of yourself as a sexual person. Use them to help you parent your daughter with her sexual health in mind at present and in the years ahead.

- Do I feel better about sex when I have more self-confidence and self-esteem?

- Have I always lived with disinterest in sex and a lack of sexual satisfaction and if so, where do I think it comes from?

- Do I feel my markers of emotional well-being are present and intact? Has this always been true or have I had to work diligently in my adult life to achieve this?

- In what ways do I help my daughter feel confident about herself?

- What do I consider to be sexy features? Why?

- Do I believe that there is a relationship between confidence and sexiness?

- Can I name anyone who is sexy and not beautiful?

THE SECRET POWER OF LETTING GO

Recently, in a row with my daughter, I said things that I deeply regretted afterward. Whenever this happens, I know I need to take some time to figure out what sent me over the edge. After giving it thought, I realized that my daughter had displayed irrefutable evidence of her growing interest in everything but me. My sadness in watching the rest of the world have more access to the best of her than I do—knowing that it's just a matter of time before I see even less of her than I do now—was at the heart of my explosive response. This is what we are supposed to encourage, but it doesn't mean we won't experience a broken heart when it actually happens.

For my daughter's sake, I went back to her, simply to state my insights and conclusion. It wasn't a topic for discussion, just an attempt to apologize for allowing my distress to take such a hurtful and negative spin. I know she appreciated what I said—that letting go is hard, but it's the right thing to do, for both of us. It's what nature intends.

My daughter becoming separate from me and my expectations and ideas of who she should be are, after all, what this book is largely about—helping mothers facilitate this process, even when it includes being sexually active and rejecting our ideas and the families we've created. These are all things that need to happen in order for our daughters to mature into healthy adult women. Despite my knowing this and writing about it, my own daughter's transition from young teen to older teen and then to young adult has been difficult for me. Her distance from me is not a reflection of her love or lack thereof; it is a reflection of her good mental health and normal development.

Helping your teenage daughter become a woman is an extraordinary process. And, no matter how distraught or pleased we end up feeling about our daughter's maturation, our experiences of mothering them through their adolescence will undoubtedly result in deep reflection on our own teenage years. How did we manage during the same period in our lives? What were the good parts, what were the bad, and what have we forgotten or remembered and why?

Raising a teen girl with an understanding and acceptance of her emerging sexuality can enlighten us about our own sexuality, body image, and sense of confidence— if we're willing to let the experience guide us in this direction. Mothering a girl is a great opportunity for reparative and restorative experiences that can mend our own wounds carried over from adolescence. There is nothing more gratifying than watching our girls experiencing the same quandaries that we faced and giving them the tools and support they need to make those conundrums less burdensome and more manageable. We can use the courage and wisdom of our life experiences, mistakes, joys, and compassion to do this.

It's impossible for any thoughtful and loving woman raising a daughter not to continually reflect on her own experiences as she watches her daughter mature. We begin from the earliest retrievable memories and advance forward along with our daughter's own aging. Despite whatever amnesia sets in, we do rely on our memories, good and bad, to guide us in parenting. Certain family patterns we either resist or repeat—sometimes without even realizing it or knowing why—and we incorporate what's new to us with what's old, hoping it will all work out for the best. Sometimes we are guided by good instincts, sometimes by old bad patterns but if we approach the situation with kindness, information, and firsthand understanding based on our own life experiences, we can raise a more sexually healthy generation of daughters, who have more access to a satisfying and rewarding sexual and relational life than we had. And isn't this the ultimate goal for all of us managing the tumultuous lives of teenage girls?

The bottom line for parents raising teens and who are concerned about their daughter's sexual health and safety is this: Face it! Your daughter's biology will drive her to separate from you to form her own identity and this may very well include making the decision to have sex with someone during adolescence. Don't wait for the school system, the government, friends, or the media to give her the information she needs to experience what's normal with a minimal amount of risk.

Give her information to read if she is reticent to talk to you and don't give up if she is shy or says, "I don't want to talk to you about this." Factual, scientifically based information from reliable sources like Planned Parenthood and the Centers for Disease Control is empowering to both of you. It provides protection from untoward consequences of sexual activity and increases the likelihood that your daughter will be safe and able to enjoy her sexuality.

People often ask me questions about my own upbringing and whether or not the language of sexuality was spoken freely in my family. The best way I can answer this is yes and no. I grew up speaking Greek before English, in a very Greek-identified home, where Greek foods, customs, and sensibilities dominated. It was a very sensual environment; meals, socializing, animals, flowers, gardening, and natural beauty were exalted, and the combination provided the perfect precursor to the development of a deep understanding of the topic and experience of sex. In combination with my natural temperament, it was easy for me to make the leap from the sensual to the sexual. The story of Aphrodite, the goddess of love and beauty—another element of my Greek heritage—not only reinforced my sexuality but also became the muse for this book.

Much like Aphrodite, who was born from the sea foam a stunningly beautiful teenager and carried over the waves to Cyprus where she became the envy of gods and goddesses alike, our teenage daughters are a symbol of wonder, awe, and fear. And like Zeus, who took one look at his daughter's sexual power and married her off to the first crippled old blacksmith he could find, our first instincts are to put a lid on all that raw desirability before something awful happens. Like the Trojan War for example.

To the early Greeks, Aphrodite was representative of the full range of human emotion, from pure and spiritual love to primal lust. As such, Aphrodite had power unlike any other god or goddess. Aphrodite was the quintessential teenage girl. Her range of emotion, her beauty, and her irresistible desirability were not simply representative of sexual attraction but were, in fact, real instruments of power that could change the world. Because of the scope and force of Aphrodite's emotional and sexual power, she was able to move with ease between her various realms of influence in the home, on the battlefield, and in the bedroom. Aphrodite expressed her passion wherever it led her, despite her father Zeus's efforts to constrain her. And in the ancient world, Aphrodite's sexual freedom was not interpreted as promiscuity.

Yet, perhaps precisely because of the threat that this vision of unbridled, unified, and ubiquitous adolescent female sexual energy represented to her parents and the world at large, Aphrodite was gradually restrained by her concerned parents, as well as the equally nervous world. Ultimately Aphrodite found herself relegated to a smaller and smaller role in the affairs of gods and men. By the time of the Roman Empire, Aphrodite had become a mere minor household goddess, confined to the realm of carnal lust and desire without any affiliation with spiritual love or higher emotion. Thus the female sexual power she represented was entirely separated from the main thrust of the female experience. This is precisely what we do to our daughters when we refuse to acknowledge or attempt to stifle their first stirrings of desire. We ultimately cut our daughters off from realizing their power as fully integrated and sexual women who can move with ease between their various realms of activity, seeking their own pleasure, and forging their own happiness.

My daughter loves to travel, and this summer, between her freshman and sophomore years in college, she has an enviable trip to Italy, Spain, and France planned. There will be three months between the time I bid her *bon voyage* and when I see her again in August. Although I know I will miss seeing her, I am thrilled for her. This trip will provide her with a great opportunity to practice her Italian and Spanish and most important to her, to enjoy the company of her sweetheart who lives much of the time in Italy. They'll enjoy one another's company and Thalia will undoubtedly expand her perspective on self, life, and love—which exactly what she's supposed to do right now. Some people who have heard about Thalia's trip have asked me if I actually feel okay about her going away for such a long period and about her being with her boyfriend so far from home. If they're wondering if I will miss her, yes. But if they're asking me if I have any hesitations about *letting* her go, absolutely not. My daughter is doing what healthy daughters of her age do; they explore the world without their parents because they have the self-confidence to do so. They also have the support of parents who know that these adventures are part of individuating and establishing yourself in the world. If I were to interfere with my daughter's plans, I would put her at risk for missing a crucial opportunity to discover more about herself, to love and feel loved, to gain independence and competence, and to learn about what makes her happy and what doesn't. Whether or not the trip leaves me feeling lonely for her or worried about her is fundamentally irrelevant. My daughter is making a conscious effort to mature, and it is my responsibility to foster this growth, especially if it includes her happiness in love.

This book is the best way I could think of to empower those of us who are raising girls and to reduce the fears so many mothers have about their daughters falling in love and becoming sexually active. It is an opportunity to continue my work to help reduce girls' and women's distress, frustration, inhibition, and sadness when it comes to sexual identity and sexual satisfaction. I intend for this to be a proclamation of reassurance to mothers about the normalcy and importance of the physical expression of love and sexual desire common in the lives of teen girls so that they better understand and accept it with less fear and more ease.

I am hopeful that the women of America—mothers, grandmothers, and young women alike—will make an effort to inform themselves about their bodies, how to stay healthy, and how to better understand the risks and benefits of living fully and sensibly in their sexuality. Learn all you can about your female body and pass the information on to other girls and women. Being knowledgeable about your body and health (your greatest assets) and how to keep them safe is a revolutionary concept in a world with so little focus on prevention of illness and distress. And in a world which does so little to teach women about the importance of sexual enjoyment and pleasure.

When it comes to sexuality, sexual health, and sexual responsibility, knowledge and facts—and the courage to speak of them—as well as a deep appreciation and understanding of the value of pleasure, is not only health enhancing but also a strong adhesive between mothers and their daughters.

We can and should grab hold of all this and pass it along from one generation of girls and women to the next. It is the healthy, sensible, and kind thing to do.

ACKNOWLEDGMENTS

Writing this book would not have been possible without the ongoing support of those who believe in what I do and the importance of my message.

Divine intervention played a hand in my meeting Bev West. She was immediately interested in my work and we started a collaboration and friendship that has been instructive, mentoring, and genuinely fun—a winning combination. She helped shape this book in many ways, and her vision for its content has been critically important in its completion. I will forever be grateful. Bev led the way to our agent, Jenny Bent, who agreed to represent us and our message. She is a courageous and very experienced agent who never ceases to impress me with her sound advice and determination. My editor at Hay House, Patty Gift, has displayed the "patience of Job" (and then some) and has guided the development of this book in the most caring and wisest of ways. Along with Laura Koch, they have never ceased to encourage me, and as a first-time author, I could not have been more fortunate, well-advised, or better cared for. Thank you, Patty and Laura for so many things far beyond the scope of this paragraph.

The work I do at Canyon Ranch in Lenox, Massachusetts, has been instrumental in solidifying the ideas for this book. Jerry Cohen, CEO, has granted me latitude and support to cultivate my message and bring my work alive. I am sure he has held his breath plenty of times, prayed and hoped for the best. Thanks, Jerry, for your acknowledgement of the importance of my work, and your support and friendship. I hope you're as satisfied with the outcome as I am.

I am so lucky to have a stellar group of colleagues from Canyon Ranch who never doubt the value of my perspective and contributions, even if they haven't always understood them. Mark Liponis and Cindy Geyer deserve special mention for their unfailing confidence in my work. Andrew Wolf advanced my insights and expanded my ways of thinking about sexuality and remains my very dear friend. Emilie Goudey has watched over me in the kindest ways while also providing great supervision. Michael Tompkins started it all by hiring me in the first place. Thank you all.

Dianne Dunkelman, founder and CEO of the The National Speaking of Women's Health Foundation played a major role in providing me with opportunities to deliver my message about sexual health to thousands of women while advancing my public speaking skills and career. Lisa Alonge has done the same for me, and her support and belief in my work have been present from the moment we met. Thank you both for everything.

John Miner, M.D., has contributed more to my success then I will ever be able to describe. His compassion, dedication, knowledge, and patience made it possible for me to take on this project and to complete it. His confidence in me is unparalleled and I have relied on it countless times; I have no words to express the depth of my gratitude.

I am deeply fortunate to have a friendship with Matthew Hock that has nourished me in all sorts of ways for over 35 years. Elements of our conversations and relationship over the years are woven throughout this book.

Carolanne McKirnan, Mark Immerman, Jean Garifallou, Cherie Stine, Jim Lobley, Mary Hall, William Sinunu, and Catriona McHardy and Renée Schultz have provided all sorts of support, encouragement, and understanding of the importance and process of my experience writing this book. Marie Brenner provided the gold standard for speaking the truth, no matter what. Thank you all.

My stepson, Nik, and my daughter have identified as siblings from the moment we became a blended family and their relationship has provided endless hilarity, pertinent information about sex and sexuality in the lives of young adults, and the importance of living with integrity as a parent.

My daughter, Thalia, is a true thoroughbred. She has taught me more than anyone else I have ever known—about all sorts of things. I have immeasurable regard and respect for her vitality, fearlessness, wit, and willingness to stand up for what she feels is right. Her resilience isn't shabby either. There is no doubt in my mind that we chose one another as mother and daughter.

My beloved, Robin, has listened to and discussed ideas with me for hours and days on end for over 15 years and in doing so, has encouraged me to accomplish so many things, including this book. We have a marriage and life filled with laughter, respect for one another and a solid commitment to continued professional, personal, and relational growth—neither of us ever takes what we have for granted. Our life together is a slice of heaven on Earth. Thanks, Rob, for absolutely everything.

Lastly, I owe my gratitude, appreciation, and respect to the thousands of girls and women who have disclosed their most painful, difficult, and joyous experiences with me. The confidence my patients have granted me has been deeply humbling and provided the insights and incentive necessary to do the work I so love doing. My heartfelt thanks to all of you, and it is my sincere hope that our work together has made it easier to claim joy and confidence in the pleasures your bodies can give you.

RESOURCES

SEXUALITY, STIs AND CONTRACEPTION INFORMATION

Websites

www.Trojancondoms.com
This is a clever, poignant, effective, and informative Website with great videos, straightforward anti-STI/pro-condom messages. Free condom samples are available for order online.

www.cdc.gov
This Website for the Centers of Disease Control will offer a multitude of information on a variety of topics. They have easy to understand fact sheets on STIs and other sexual health topics that are available to download and print and are appropriate for teens and their parents.

www.plannedparenthood.org
This site offers comprehensive information on contraceptives and STI prevention. Also, you can find the location of the Planned Parenthood office nearest you.

www.familiesaretalking.org
This Website has been designed and created by the Sexuality Information and Education Council of the United States (SIECUS) specifically to help parents talk with their kids about sex. They have helpful suggestions and infor-

mation about starting and maintaining conversations with your kids about sex designed to keep communication open between parents and kids.

www.positive.org
This is the site for the Coalition for Positive Sexuality. Information is sexual health and sex positive in style and content. It may feel a bit edgy to some, but its content is real, honest, no-nonsense talk for teens and their parents and contains comprehensive and accurate information about the risks and benefits of being sexually active.

www.sexetc.org
This site is written by teens, for teens and features clear and honest answers to questions most asked and ideas most often shared among teens and their friends. This is an extremely informative and helpful resource for parents who want the real lowdown on what their teens and friends are talking about.

www.teenwire.com
This is an excellent site with comprehensive information on all sorts of sex-specific topics and concerns, sponsored by Planned Parenthood.

Books

Pardes, Bronwen. *Doing it Right: Making Smart, Safe, and Satisfying Choices about Sex*. New York: Simon Pulse, 2007.

Bell, Ruth. *Changing Bodies, Changing Lives.* New York: Random House, 1998.

Harris, Robie. *It's Perfectly Normal: Changing Bodies, Growing up, Sex, and Sexual Health.* Sommerville, Massachusetts: Candlewick Press, 2004.

BODY IMAGE & EATING DISORDERS

Websites

www.AdiosBarbie.com
This is a fantastic site that helps girls and women love their bodies, no matter the size. Great videos, books, news updates, and healthy approaches to loving the skin you're in and staying healthy.

www.nationaleatingdisorders.org
This is the Website of the National Eating Disorders Association, which provides information about eating disorders and how to get help.

www.bodypositive.com
This is a great site for ideas on boosting body image at any weight. This site is sponsored by the Our Bodies, Our Selves Coalition that publishes the book by the same title as well as others worth reading and having.

www.campaignforrealbeauty.com
A site conceived and managed by Dove beauty products

which are changing the way we all look at beauty. Have must-see videos on the impact of the beauty industry and advertising on girls and women's images of their bodies and themselves. An excellent site for girls and their mothers to explore.

www.Bulimia.com
A wide selection of eating disorders publications and additional information.

Weight Control Information Network
Provides helpful information on prevention and identification of obesity in kids.
http://win.niddk.gov/publications/child.htm
877-946-4627

Films

THIN
HBO documentary directed by acclaimed contemporary photographer Lauren Greenfield. Greenfield looks at the real life stories of 4 women in a treatment center for eating disorders. Intense, real, and critically valuable.

Books

Edut, Ophira. *Body Outlaws: Rewriting the Rules about Beauty and Body Image.* California: Seal Press, 2003.

RELATIONSHIPS, DATING & TEEN LIFE

Websites

www.teenvoices.com
This is a fantastic magazine online and in hard copy written by, for and about real teenage girls. Terrific content and very different from trade teen magazines.

www.gurl.com
This is a great Website covering many aspects of teen life.

Books

Drill, Esther, McDonald, Heather, and Odes, Rebecca. *Deal With It*. Pocket Books, 1999.

PARENTING GIRLS

Books

The Mother-Daughter Project. Sue Ellen Hamkins and Renée Schultz. Hudson Street Press, New York 2007.

ENDNOTES

INTRODUCTION

1. CDC, "Youth Risk Behavior Surveillance Survey (YRBSS)," http://apps.nccd.cdc.gov/yrbss/Quest YearTable.asp?path=byHT&ByVar=CI&cat=4&quest=Q58&year=2007&loc=XX (accessed November 3, 2008)
2. Guttmacher Institute, "U.S. Teenage Pregnancy Statistics national and State Trends and Trends by Race and Ethnicity," 2.

CHAPTER 1

1. Goleman, Social Intelligence, 244.
2. Lewis, Amini, and Lannon, A General Theory of Love, 77.

CHAPTER 2

1. Tanner, You're Wearing That?, 35
2. Flynn, "What's the Perfect Look?," Question 4, http://www.teenwire.com/interactive/quizzes/do-20030403-beauty.php (accessed 12/3/08)
3. Girl Scout Research Institute, "The Ten Emerging Truths," 9.
4. Eating Disorders Coalition, Fact Sheet, http://www.eatingdisorderscoalition.org/documents/

TalkingpointsEatingDisordersFactSheet.pdf
(accessed September 1, 2008)

5. ANAD, "ANAD Fact Sheet," http://www.anad.
    org/5148/525801.html (accessed September 7,
    2008)

6. NIMH, "Eating Disorders," Pages 5–6, http://
    www.nimh.nih.gov/health/publications/eating-
    disorders/nimheatingdisorders.pdf (accessed
    March 18, 2009)

7. AP, "Study Says Mothers May Pass On Eating
    Disorders," http://query.nytimes.com/gst/fullpage.
    html?sec=health&res=9D0CE4DE143BF936A3575
    6C0A967958260# (accessed September 2, 2008)

8. NIMH, "Eating Disorders," Pages 7–9, http://
    www.nimh.nih.gov/health/publications/eating-
    disorders/nimheatingdisorders.pdf (accessed
    March 18, 2009)

9. AAP, "Expert Committee Releases Recommenda-
    tions To Fight Childhood And Adolescent Obe
    sity," www.aap.org/advocacy/releases/june07obe
    sity.htm, (accessed November 19, 2008)

10. Lamb and Brown, Packaging Girlhood, 33.

11. Lamb and Brown, Packaging Girlhood, 48.

12. CDC, "National Vital Statistics Report Births:
    Final Data for 2002," http://www.cdc.gov/nchs/
    pressroom/02news/ameriwomen.htm (accessed
    November 20, 2008)

CHAPTER 4

1. Men Against Sexual Assault, "Sexual Assault Statistics," http://sa.rochester.edu/masa/stats.php (accessed February 2, 2009)
2. Sullivan, "Over 3 Million Teen Girls Infected with STDs," 12.
3. Guttmacher Institute, "U.S. Teenage Pregnancy Statistics national and State Trends and Trends by Race and Ethnicity," 3
4. Sullivan, "Over 3 Million Teen Girls Infected with STDs," 12.
5. Partnership to End Cervical Cancer, "Human Papillomavirus (HPV) and Cervical Cancer," http://www.nocervicalcancer.org/hpv_cc_faqs.html.
6. Winer, "Risk of Female Human Papillomavirus Acquisition Associated with First Male Sex Partner," 279.
7. Winer, R. et. al, "Condom Use and the Risk of Genital Human Papillomavirus Infection in Young Women," http://content.nejm.org/cgi/content/full/354/25/2645.
8. Sullivan, Michael G. "Over 3 Million Teen Girls Infected with STDs," 12.
9. CDC, "Sexually Transmitted Disease Surveillance 2007," http://www.cdc.gov/std/stats07/chlamydia.htm (accessed September 3, 2008)
10. Davis, "Chlamydia Screening in Young Women: Are We Missing the Boat?" 55

11. Kriebs, "Understanding Herpes Simplex Virus: Transmission, Diagnosis and Considerations in Pregnancy Management," 203.
12. Ibid, 203.
13. Miner. "We're Here. We're Sexual. Get used to it," 22.

Chapter 5

1. Goleman, *Social Intelligence,* 44-45, 60-61.
2. Guttmacher Institiute, "Facts on American Teens' Sexual and Reproductive Health," 3.
3. Brizendine, *Female Brain,* 35.
4. Simmons, *Odd Girl Out,* 243.

Chapter 6

1. Goleman, Daniel, from a lecture at Kripalu: Center for Health & Yoga, Stockbridge, MA: December 2007.

Chapter 7

1. Paolucci, E.O., Genuia, M.L., and Violato, C., "A Meta-Analysis of the Published Research on the Effects of Child Abuse," 18.

BIBLIOGRAPHY

Adios Barbie: A Body Lovin' Site for EVERY Body, www.adiosbarbie.com

American Academy of Pediatrics (AAP). "Expert Committee Releases Recommendations to Fight Childhood and Adolescent Obesity," press release, http://www.aap.org/advocacy/releases/june07obesity.htm

AP, "Study Says Mothers May Pass On Eating Disorders," *New York Times*, May 5, 1991, http://query.nytimes.com/gst/fullpage.html?sec=health&res=9D0CE4DE143BF936A35756C0A967958260#

Behrendt, Greg and Liz Tuccillo. *He's Just Not That Into You: The No Excuses Truth to Understanding Guys.* New York, NY: Simon & Schuster, 2004.

Blakemore, S.J. "Development of the Social Brain During Adolescence," *Quarterly Journal of Experimental Psychology* 61, no. 1 (January 2008): 40–49.

Body Positive: Boosting Body Image at Any Weight, www.bodypositive.com

Bouris, Karen. *The First Time: What Parents & Teenage Girls Should Know about "Losing Your Virginity."* New York: Conari Press, 1995.

Brady, Sonya S. and Halpern-Flesher, Bonnie L. "Social and Emotional Consequences of Refraining from Sexual Activity Among Sexually Experienced and Inexperienced Youths in California." *American Journal of Public Health* (January 2008): 162–168.

Brizendine, Louann. *The Female Brain.* New York: Morgan Road Books, 2007.

Burlock, Anita, and Koniak-Griffin, Deborah. "Health Care Access, Sexually Transmitted Diseases and Adolescents: Identifying Barriers and Creating Solutions." *Journal of Pediatric Nursing* (October 2002): 320–329.

Centers for Disease Control and Prevention. "Fact Sheet: HIV/AIDS Among Youth," Revised August 2008, http://www.cdc.gov/hiv/resources/factsheets/youth.htm

_____. "Sexually Transmitted Disease Surveillance 2007." http://www.cdc.gov/std/stats07/

_____. "Physical Dating Violence Among High School Students-United States, 2003." http://www.cdc.org.gov/mmwr/preview/mmwrhtml/mm5519a3.htm

_____. "National Vital Statistics Report Births: Final Data for 2002," Report by the National Center for Health Statistics, December 17, 2003, http://www.cdc.gov/nchs/pressroom/02news/ameriwomen.htm

_____. "Human Papillomavirus: HPV Information for Clinicians" (April 2007): 1–31.

_____. "Recent Trends in Teenage Pregnancy in the United States, 1990–2002," report by the National Center for Health Statistics. December 2006. http://www.cdc.gov/nchs/products/pubs/pubd/hestats/teenpreg1990-2002/teenpreg1990-2002.htm

_____. "Youth Risk Behavior Surveillance Survey (YRBSS)," http://www.cdc.gov/healthyyouth/yrbs/index.htm

Coleman, Eli. "Creating a Sexually Healthier World through Effective Public Policy." *International Journal of Sexual Health* 19, no. 3 (2007): 5–24.

Cozolino, Louis. *The Neuroscience of Human Relationships: Attachment and the Developing Social Brain.* New York, London: W.W. Norton & Company, 2006.

Davis, Ann J. "Chlamydia Screening in Young Women: Are We Missing the Boat?" *Journal Watch Women's Health* (July 2008): 55.

Dodson, Betty. *Sex for One: The Joy of Selfloving.* New York, NY: Three Rivers Press, 1996.

Eating Disorders Coalition: For Research, Policy & Action, www.eatingdisorderscoalition.org.

Flanagan, Caitlin. "What Girls Want." *The Atlantic* (December 2008): 108–120.

Flynn, Katharine. "What's the Perfect Look?" Beauty perception quiz, teenwire.com, http://www.teenwire.com/interactive/quizzes/do-20030403-beauty.php

Frankel, Loren. "An Appeal for Additional Research about the Development of Heterosexual Male Sexual Identity." *Journal of Psychology and Human Sexuality* 16, no. 4 (2004): 1–16.

Girl Scout Research Institute. "The Ten Emerging Truths: New Directions for Girls 11–17, Executive Summary," 2006, Girl Scouts Overview of the Truths, 9.

Goleman, Daniel. *Emotional Intelligence: Why It Can Matter More than IQ*. New York: Bantam, 1995.

_____. *Social Intelligence: The Revolutionary New Science of Human Relationships*. New York: Bantam, 2007.

Gurian, Michael. *The Wonder of Girls: Understanding the Hidden Nature of Our Daughters*. New York: Simon & Schuster, Limited, 2003.

Guttmacher Institute. "U.S. Teenage Pregnancy Statistics National and State Trends and Trends by Race and Ethnicity." (September 2006): 1–9.

_____."Facts on American Teens' Sexual and Reproductive Health." http://www.gutmacher.org/pubs/fb_ATSRH.html.

Greenfield, Lauren. "THIN." http://www.lauren greenfield.com/index.php?p=Y6QZZ990

Haffner, Debra W. *Beyond the Big Talk: Every Parent's Guide to Raising Sexually Healthy Teens—From Middle School to High School and Beyond.* New York: Newmarket Press, 2002.

_____. *What Every 21st-Century Parent Needs to Know: Facing Today's Challenges with Wisdom and Heart.* New York: Newmarket Press, 2008.

Hamkins, SuEllen and Renée Schultz. *The Mother-Daughter Project: How Mothers and Daughters Can Band Together, Beat the Odds, and Thrive Through Adolescence.* New York: Hudson Street Press, 2007.

Harris, Robie, H. *It's Perfectly Normal: Changing Bodies, Growing Up, Sex, and Sexual Health.* Massachusetts, Candlewick Press, 1996.

Hatcher, Juliet L. and Scarpa, Juliet. "Encouraging Teens to Adopt a Safe, Healthy Lifestyle: A Foundation for Improving Future Adult Behaviors," June 2002, Trends Child Research Brief, www.childtrends.org

Heavy., et al "Difference in Pregnancy Desire among Pregnant Female Adolescents at a State-funded Family Planning Clinic." *Journal of Midwifery and Women's Health* (March/April 2008): 130–137.

Jukes, Mavis and Cheung, Lilian. *Be Healthy! It's a Girl Thing: Food, fitness and feeling great.* New York: Crown Books, 2003.

Kearney-Cooke, Ann. *Change Your Mind, Change Your Body: Feeling good about your body and self after 40.* New York: Atria Books, 2004.

Kim, YS Sue. "Nature Versus Nurture in Childhood Obesity: A Familiar Old Conundrum," December 2003 http://www.acjn.org/cgi/content/full78/6/1051 (accessed December 28, 2008)

Kitzinger, Sheila. *Woman's Experience of Sex: The Facts and Feelings of Female Sexuality at Every Stage of Life.* New York: Penguin Books, 1983.

Kriebs, Jan M. "Understanding Herpes Simplex Virus: Transmission, Diagnosis, and Considerations in Pregnancy Management." *Journal of Midwifery and Women's Health* (May/June 2008): 202–208.

Lamb, S. and Brown, L. M. *Packaging Girlhood: Rescuing Our Daughter from Marketers Schemes.* New York: St. Martin's Press, 2006.

Lewis, Thomas, Fari Amini, and Richard Lannon. *A General Theory of Love.* New York: Vintage, 2001.

Luker, Kristin. *When Sex Goes to School.* New York: Norton, 2006.

Mahoney, Diana. "Pap Testing Not Necessary in Most Adolescents." *Internal Medicine News* (April 2008): 13.

Marelich, William D. and Lundquist, Jessica. "Motivations for Sexual Intimacy: Development of a Needs-Based Sexual Intimacy Scale." *International Journal of Sexual Health* 20, no. 3 (2008): 177–186.

Melby, Todd. "The Myth of Teen Promiscuity." *Contemporary Sexuality* (September 2008): 1–5.

Men Against Sexual Assault. "Sexual Assault Statistics," http://sa.rochester.edu/masa/stats.php

Miner, Barbara. "We're Here. We're Sexual. Get used to it." *Colorlines* (May/June 2008): 19–28.

National Association for Anorexia Nervosa and Associated Eating Disorders (ANAD). www.anad.org

National Association for Self Esteem (NASE). "Self Esteem Booster." http://www.self-esteem-nase.org/booster.php (accessed September 9, 2008)

National Institute of Mental Health (NIMH). "Eating Disorders," Informational booklet of facts about eating disorders, http://www.nimh.nih.gov/health/publications/eating-disorders/nimheatingdisorders.pdf

National Organization for Women (NOW). "Violence Against Women in the United States: Statistics." http://www.now.org/issues/violence/stats.html

"New Youth Survey is 'Troubling.'" *Contemporary Sexuality* (August 2008): 8.

Northrup, Christiane. *Mother Daughter Wisdom; Creating a Legacy of Physical and Emotional Health.* New York: Bantam, 2003.

Office of the Surgeon General, "The Surgeon General's Call to Action to Promote Sexual Health and Responsible Sexual Behavior." Rockville, Maryland, 2001.

Ogden, Gina. *Women Who Love Sex: Ordinary Women Describe Their Paths to Pleasure, Intimacy, and Ecstasy.* Boston: Shambhala/Trumpeter, 2007.

Ogden, Jane and Steward, Jo. "The Role of Mother-Daughter Relationships in Explaining Weight Concerns." *International Journal of Eating Disorders* 28, no. 1 (May 2000): 78–83.

Paolucci, E.O. and Genuia, M.L. and Violato, C. "A Meta-Analysis of the Published Research on the Effects of Child Abuse." *The Journal of Psychology* 135, no. 11 (January 2001): 17–37.

Pardes, Bronwen. *Doing It Right: Making Smart, Safe, and Satisfying Choices about Sex.* New York: Simon Pulse, 2007.

Partnership to End Cervical Cancer, http://www.nocervicalcancer.org/

Perel, Esther. *Mating in Captivity: Reconciling the Erotic + the Domestic.* New York: HarperCollins, 2006.

Pipher, Mary. *Reviving Ophelia: Saving the Selves of Adolescent Girls.* New York: Ballantine Books, 1994.

Prescott, Margaret E. and LePoire, Beth A. "Eating Disorders and Mother-Daughter Communication: A Test of Inconsistent Nurturing." *Journal of Family Communication* 2 (January 2002): 59–78.

Planned Parenthood. "The Health Benefits of Sexual Expression." http:www.plannedparenthood.org/news-articles-press/politics-policy-issues/medcial-sex

Price, Kate. Letter to the editor, *Sun Magazine* 343 (July 2004).

Regan, C. Pamela, et al. "Fireworks Exploded in My Mouth: Affective Responses Before, During and After the Very First Kiss." *International Journal of Sexual Health* 19, no. 2 (2007): 1–16.

Richardson, Justin and Schuster, Mark. *Everything You Never Wanted Your Kids to Know About Sex (But Were Afraid They'd Ask).* New York: Three Rivers Press, 2003.

Romano, J. "Q&A Dr. Kathleen Pike: Challenging the Must-Be-Thin Message." *New York Times,* (February 23, 1992): http://www.nytimes.com/1992/02/23/nyregion/new-jersey-q-a-dr-kathleen-pike-challenging-the-must-be-thin-message.html?sec=health (accessed 2/3/09)

Rothschild, Babette. *The Body Remembers: The Psychophysiology of Trauma and Trauma Treatment.* Boston: W. W. Norton & Company, Incorporated, 2000.

Santelli, et al. "Explaining Recent Declines in Adolescent Pregnancy in the United States: The Contribution of Abstinence and Improved Condom Use." *American Journal of Public Health* (January 2007): 150–156.

Sapolsky, Robert M. *Why Zebras Don't Get Ulcers.* New York: St. Martin's Press, 2004.

Sato, S.M., et al. "Adolescents and Androgens, Receptors and Rewards." *Hormones and Behavior.* (May 2008): 647–658.

Schneider, Mary Ellen. "Teenage Birth Rate Increases; Sex Education Delays Debut." *Internal Medicine News* (April 2008): 12.

Sexuality Information and Education Council of the United States (SIECUS). *Guidelines for Comprehensive Sexuality Education—Kindergarten through Grade 12, 3rd Edition.* (New York: Fulton Press, 2004).

_____. "Teen Pregnancy, Birth and Abortion." September 28, 2006, SIECUS, http://ww.siecus.org/pubs/fact/fact0010.html (accessed September 2007)

_____. "The Truth About Adolescent Sexuality." August 8, 2007, SIECUS, http://www.siecus.org/pubs/fact/fact0020. html (accessed September 2007).

Shandler, Sara. *Ophelia Speaks: Adolescent Girls Write about Their Search for Self.* New York: Harper Perennial, 1999.

Simmons, Rachel. *Odd Girl Out: The Hidden Culture of Aggression in Girls.* New York: Harcourt Trade, 2002.

St-Onge, Marie-Pierre, Keller, Kathleen L., and Heymfield, Steven B. "Changes in Childhood Food Consumption Patterns: A Cause for Concern in Light of Increasing Body Weights." *American Journal of Clinical Nutrition* 78, no. 6 (December 2003): 1068–1073. http://www. ajcn.org/cgi/content/full/78/6/1068

Sullivan, Michael G. "Over 3 Million Teen Girls Infected with STDs." *Internal Medicine News* (April 2008): 12.

Swain, R. Carolyn and Ackerman, K. Lynn, and Ackerman, Mark. "The Influence of Individual Characteristics and Contraceptive Beliefs on Parent-Teen Communications: A Structural Model." *Journal of Adolescent Health* 38 (June 2006): 753–757.

Talbot, Margaret. "Red Sex, Blue Sex," November 3, 2008. *The New Yorker,* http://www.newyorker.com/ reporting/2008/11/03/081103fa_fact_talbot

Tannen, Deborah. *You're Wearing That?: Understanding Mothers and Daughters in Conversation.* New York: Ballantine Books, 2006.

Thompson, Sharon. "Putting a Big Thing into a Little Hole: Teenage Girls' Accounts of Sexual Initiation." *Journal of Sex Research* 27 (1990): 341–61.

Tolman, Deborah L. *Dilemmas of Desire: Teenage Girls Talk about Sexuality.* New York: Harvard University Press, 2002.

Wald, Anna. "HPV Does Not Respect Monogamy." *Journal Watch Women's Health* (May 2008): 39.

Weinstein, Rebecca, B. and Walsh, Jennifer L. Ward, L. Monique. "Testing a New Measure of Sexual Health Knowledge and its Connections to Students' Sex Education, Communication, Confidence, and Condom Use." *International Journal of Sexual Health* 20, no. 3 (2008) 212–221.

Weiss, David, and Bullough, Vern L. "Adolescent American Sex." *Journal of Psychology and Human Sexuality* 16, no. 2/3 (2004): 43–53.

Willett, Walter. *Eat, Drink and be Healthy: The Harvard Medical School Guide to Healthy Eating.* Boston: Free Press, 2005.

Winer, R. et al. "Condom Use and the Risk of Genital Human Papillomavirus Infection in Young Women."

New England Journal of Medicine 354, no. 25 (June 22, 2006), http://content.nejm.org/cgi/content/full/354/25/2645

_____. "Risk of Female Human Papillomavirus Acquisition Associated with First Male Sex Partner." *Journal of Infectious Disease* 197, no. 2 (January 2008) 279–282.

Wolf, Naomi. *Promiscuities: The Secret Struggle for Womanhood.* New York: Random House Canada, 1997.

Yurgelen, Todd D. Emotional and Cognitive Changes During Adolescence. *Current Opinion in Neurobiology* 17, no. 2 (April 2007): 251–257.

Zonfrillo, Nancy J. and Hackley, Barbara. "The Quadrivalent Human Papillomavirus Vaccine: Potential Factors in Effectiveness," *Journal of Midwifery and Women's Health* 53, no. 3 (May/June 2008): 188–194.

ABOUT THE AUTHORS

Evelyn Resh, CNM, MPH, has been in practice as a certified nurse-midwife for over 20 years. She is also a certified sexuality counselor with the American Association of Sexuality Educators, Counselors and Therapists.

Evelyn holds a Master's of Public Health degree from Boston University School of Public Health and undergraduate degrees in nursing from Greenfield Community College, and in psychology and medical anthropology from Mt. Holyoke College. She practices integrative midwifery and gynecology with women of all ages and lectures frequently throughout the nation to professional and lay audiences on the topics of women's health and sexual satisfaction. She is especially known for her warm, lively, and good-humored approach to her subject matter and her ability to make others feel comfortable with often hard-to-discuss topics.

Evelyn is currently the director of sexual health services and programming for Canyon Ranch Health Resort in Lenox, Massachusetts. In her role as director, she creates and implements programming focusing on the integration of sensuality into daily living as well as the improvement of sexual satisfaction for individuals and couples of all sexual orientations and ages

Evelyn lives in western Massachusetts with her family where she also maintains a small private practice as a sexuality counselor. You can visit her Website at: **www.evelynresh.com.**

Beverly West is the co-author of the best-selling *Cinematherapy* series, which inspired the program on WE tv. She is the author of many books, including six with her husband, Jason Bergund, including the Booksense bestseller *What Pets Do While You're at Work, Pugtherapy,* and their latest, *Please Don't Feed the Daisy: Living, Loving, and Losing Weight with the World's Hungriest Dog.* Beverly lives on her urban farm on the Upper West Side of Manhattan with her husband and their four dogs, one cat, two turtles, and two glorious gardens.

NOTES

NOTES

NOTES

NOTES

NOTES

Hay House Titles of Related Interest

YOU CAN HEAL YOUR LIFE, the movie,
starring Louise L. Hay & Friends
(available as a 1-DVD program and an expanded 2-DVD set)
Watch the trailer at: **www.LouiseHayMovie.com**

THE SHIFT, the movie,
starring Dr. Wayne W. Dyer
(available as a 1-DVD program and an expanded 2-DVD set)
Watch the trailer at: **www.DyerMovie.com**

***

THE ART OF EXTREME SELF-CARE:
Transform Your Life One Month at a Time,
by Cheryl Richardson

THE LAST DROPOUT: Stop the Epidemic!
by Bill Milliken

THE LIVES OUR MOTHERS LEAVE US:
Prominent Women Discuss the Complex,
Humorous, and Ultimately Loving Relationships
They Have with Their Mothers,
by Patti Davis

A VERY HUNGRY GIRL:
How I Filled Up on Life . . . and How You Can, Too!
by Jessica Weiner

WHAT IS YOUR SELF-WORTH?:
A Woman's Guide to Validation,
by Cheryl Saban, Ph.D.

***

All of the above are available at your local bookstore,
or may be ordered by contacting Hay House (see next page).

We hope you enjoyed this Hay House book.
If you'd like to receive our online catalog featuring additional
information on Hay House books and products,
or if you'd like to find out more about the
Hay Foundation, please contact:

Hay House, Inc.
P.O. Box 5100
Carlsbad, CA 92018-5100

(760) 431-7695 or **(800) 654-5126**
(760) 431-6948 (fax) or **(800) 650-5115 (fax)**
www.hayhouse.com® • **www.hayfoundation.org**

***

Published and distributed in Australia by: Hay House Australia Pty.
Ltd., 18/36 Ralph St., Alexandria NSW 2015 • *Phone:* 612-9669-4299
Fax: 612-9669-4144 • www.hayhouse.com.au

Published and distributed in the United Kingdom by: Hay House
UK, Ltd., 292B Kensal Rd., London W10 5BE
Phone: 44-20-8962-1230 • *Fax:* 44-20-8962-1239
www.hayhouse.co.uk

Published and distributed in the Republic of South Africa by:
Hay House SA (Pty), Ltd., P.O. Box 990, Witkoppen 2068 • *Phone/Fax:*
27-11-467-8904 • info@hayhouse.co.za • www.hayhouse.co.za

Published in India by: Hay House Publishers India, Muskaan
Complex, Plot No. 3, B-2, Vasant Kunj, New Delhi 110 070 • *Phone:*
91-11-4176-1620 • *Fax:* 91-11-4176-1630 • www.hayhouse.co.in

Distributed in Canada by: Raincoast, 9050 Shaughnessy St.,
Vancouver, B.C. V6P 6E5 • *Phone:* (604) 323-7100
Fax: (604) 323-2600 • www.raincoast.com

***

<u>Take Your Soul on a Vacation</u>

Visit **www.HealYourLife.com®** to regroup, recharge, and reconnect
with your own magnificence. Featuring blogs, mind-body-spirit
news, and life-changing wisdom from Louise Hay and friends.

Visit **www.HealYourLife.com** today!